UNRAVELING PASSION
CONFRONT YOUR PAST TO FIND YOUR FUTURE

PRISCILLA SMITH

CONTENTS

To my family, who have been my sounding board and source of encouragement.

To all the people who have been a part of my life, who have supported me, inspired me, and helped me to become the person I am today.

And to you, dear reader, thank you for taking the time to read my book, I hope it brings you as much joy as it brought me to write it.

With gratitude,
Priscilla Smith

INTRODUCTION

You've been told a lie. Everything you've been told about facing your past is wrong. In fact, you know you've heard it before, people telling you don't look back look ahead or forget your past and move on.

The truth is, you've tried to face your past. The dark past you dare not tell others about because you don't want to be judged or looked at differently by family and friends. It's the experiences you faced alone, the times where the silence was so loud you couldn't concentrate. You wanted to run away but you were trapped. You were stuck in your environment with no escape.

For thirty years I was paralyzed by my past. So much so that it was impossible to accept any successes in my life. Have you ever felt like the best part of your life and your purpose was right under your nose but because you didn't know how to confront your past, you couldn't see it? Did you feel blind? Like there was a dark canopy that followed you around and you couldn't escape it?

Imagine for a moment if you knew how to confront your past. When I say confront, I'm not just talking about facing your past, there is a difference. I'm talking about unraveling it, undoing all the twists and knots that has been holding you captive. How would you feel if you weren't stuck anymore? Wouldn't it be amazing to let it all out and finally, breathe?

I'm going to show you precisely how to do this. You will not only learn the steps, but you will experience each step I took to live this out in my life. The lies I've been told all these years about facing my past hindered me from experiencing life to the fullest. Your family shouldn't have to duplicate the cycle any longer because the cycle stops with you, today. Like it stopped for me.

My name is Priscilla Smith, I've been running from my past for thirty years. It wasn't until October 2020 that I confronted it head on. After the collision, it took another two years of me fighting myself so that I could find myself. I'm a business owner, a founder of an amazing nonprofit and creator of a luxury bath and body product line. For many years I've had the privilege of helping my team find themselves in a beautiful way. Part of the healing process for me was writing this book. This is not a business book, it's not a book of unrealistic expectations either. You will not get a fuzzy fantasy feeling about how easy it is to confront your past. It's a book that outlines my life's journey in re-finding myself after the mess I made of my life. It's raw. My struggles were loud, unapologetic and in my face to say the least.

Before you flip the page, first let's start by addressing the elephant in the room. Before you can find yourself, let me ask you a question. Have you ever wondered or asked yourself why you were born into your family? Do you want to see why this very question is one of the keys to unraveling and confronting your past? Good, now you're ready to read my story.

1

WHO ARE YOU?

IT HAPPENS TO ALL OF US

You wake up early in the morning; the day hasn't even started, and you're already tired. Maybe you have a long list of things to do at work, or you have a ton of assignments to turn in to your university. Or perhaps, after you get the kids off to school, you have chores that need to get done.

Whatever it is, the fact is you're buried in commitments, and you're exhausted.

Finally, after a long day, the evening arrives, and it's time to wind down. The phone, which is faced down on your nightstand, suddenly rings. You pick it up, look at it, and, for a few seconds, think to yourself, *Awe crap. I don't have time for this right now, what has my brother, sister or close friend gotten into this time?* You instantly feel frustrated, anxious, and uneasy because you know what's about to happen; it's happened dozens of times before—the long, drawn-out conversation with the person calling you. It never fails. They complain about situations you can't control.

No matter what you say, nothing changes. Any piece of advice you give them goes in one ear and out the other. Your opinion doesn't matter anyway, so what's the point? You do everything in your power to ignore the call but then you start to wonder if it's an emergency. So, you cave in. You angrily answer. "Hello!" After a few minutes of catching up, it starts. The pity party of circumstances that, frankly, are all avoidable. You start to feel like a broken record, so you don't say much of anything. You let them speak freely, but coming from you is a simple:

- Oh, I see.
- Yeah, that's true.
- Man, I'm sorry.
- It'll get better.
- Ok, well hang in there.

When you hang up the phone, you shake your head and think, *Wow. Do they see the insanity? Their life is like a sad, dejected movie that makes them feel miserable. Clearly, they're unhappy with their lifestyle. The negativity is so intense they can't see straight. Day in and day out, they hit low after low, yet they don't understand why this is happening to them. It's appalling.*

Let's play this out for a moment. The example that was just shared about the phone call with a family member can essentially be perceived two different ways. You are either the person making the call or the person answering the call. As you read along, you must ask yourself two questions; is it me? Am I the one making the call? Am I the one that needs help? Or is it them? Is my role in this scenario the person that is receiving the call? Am I the one that is tired of trying to help?

One thing we all know to be true is that in this universe, no one chooses the family they're born into. It doesn't matter what part of the world you are from: your race, ethnicity, or sex; even your beliefs and political affiliations. The reality is your family is chosen for you.

Even though we don't get to choose our families, our job as humans is to learn who we are and understand that we are to leave behind our truths for the next generation. But before we can learn about ourselves, at some point we may have considered asking this very question—Why was I born into my family? Perhaps you've wondered why you were born in this era, or why you were even born at all. Conceivably, you ask yourself these questions because there was a time in your life when you felt invisible, disregarded, or out of control, as if you weren't in touch with who you are as a person and had difficulty aligning yourself with others.

Especially family.

Don't feel bad; it's easy to judge family members. After all, you don't think like they do; in fact, you're not like them at all. You're different. You're struggling with your own issues and fighting your own battles. It appears like your obligations keep piling up but you're still trying. Why can't they? You don't have an option to be irresponsible because there are people relying on you. And if you're being honest, they have people relying on them too, but they don't seem to care. It's hard to feel sorry for someone that accepts the absurdity in their lives, yet still somehow expects you to have the answers to their self-inflicted problems. They make it easy to judge them.

How many times have you wished you had a different family? But wishing you had a different family essentially means you're wishing you didn't know them at all. Isn't that an awful thing to think? The truth is, it's horrifying to consider that you never knew your family and the times you had those thoughts it made you feel terrible. I mean, who says that? That's insane. The mere definition of insanity says it all, doing the same thing over and over and expecting a different result. You want to help your family, but you just don't know how. As infuriating as they may be, you still love them. You're not trying to be nefarious; you simply don't know how to change the circumstances they unearth for themselves.

3

IS IT ME?

If you haven't experienced a call with a family member like this before, perhaps you're the person making the call. You're the one with the self-inflicted problems who's looking for answers.

You tried calling friends, but it didn't work because they wouldn't give you any advice. They told you to ignore anyone that had the audacity to tell you what to do. They encouraged you to snub family's opinions because it steals the fun out of your life. "Just be you," they said. "You're special. Your family doesn't understand you. If they can't accept you, ignore them and do what makes you happy."

However, one of the problems with advice from friends like this is they often overlook the obvious that you're in desperate need of help! And no matter where you turn, you can't seem to find it. Discounting loved ones happens often because we feel like we're not good enough. It's as if we're being told to be like them, to live like them, and to think like them. But we're not them!

For some of you, family is all you have. Real friends are few and far between. You discovered that friends are often not your friends at all. You're no stranger to that one "friend" that told you they would be there for you. Then as soon as they no longer benefited from having you around, they left. So, family has become the only people you can talk to. But at times, even that doesn't feel promising.

If this, is you, you're exhausted. You feel like your voice means nothing, and you've gotten used to having broken relationships. You're down on yourself and feel like you were set up to fail. You're stuck! Nothing you do is working anymore.

You're completely in over your head, and although you try your best to fit in, it's never good enough.

Each one of us deal with problems differently. Some of us may drink alcohol or try different types of drugs to cope. Or if drinking and drugging isn't your thing, maybe you just sleep. At least when you're sleeping, your mind is free. But no matter what you do, the reality of your life fails to escape you. You feel ashamed and degraded, like you're nothing. You're enslaved by daily burdens; you're enslaved by anxiety and depression, and by the fear of what your future will bring. You feel useless, incapable, and unworthy and like there's no way out. You can't endure the burden any longer. You just want to SCREAM! Deep down, you want to change, but you have no power, so you accept that things won't get any better.

Then something in you says, "This is not the way to live life. This can't be the way to live life. Right?"

You want so bad for your family to understand you.

You wish they would offer a simple enough solution you can apply to your life. You can't explain it, but your brain works different than theirs. You hear what they're saying, but when it comes time to devise a plan, you shut down. You lose sight of what matters because you get lost in the details of what it takes to change. There are too many steps. Your body is drained just thinking about it because it doesn't seem practical. So instead, you instantly feel paralyzed.

Let's be honest: living like this really sucks. Even though you're thankful for the family and friends you have, the situation really sucks, and you hate everything about it.

IS IT THEM?

On the other hand, being the person on the receiving side of the call from that family member, believe it or not, there are stages to your anguish. You can remember in the beginning you were all ears. You had a grave concern for their problems and tried everything you could to help. But then the weeks turned to months, the months to years, and nothing you suggested worked. They didn't listen, yet kept calling for help. Life for you was becoming harder and busier in general that you eventually lost the ability to feel sorry for them because they didn't want to help themselves.

No matter what these stages look like for you, it's still heartbreaking to see family in utter chaos. It's lonely! You feel secluded. You tried isolating yourself so you can think clearly, as if somehow, by doing that, you will find a way to get through to them. You have the means and resources to help them, but you feel like no one on earth will ever understand why you don't. But in all honesty, you can't help them because if you do, you'll be enabling them to stay in that condition. When will they wake up and stop relying on others to fix their situation?

IT'S NOT YOUR FAULT

No matter which side of the call you're on understand that it's not your fault. It's said that our childhood experiences shape who we become as adults. For some of us, our childhoods were amazing. We vacationed with family, ate good food, and genuinely enjoyed each other's company. For others, life was a little harder. Although we had food to eat and a place to live, we didn't get the pleasure of traveling or doing fun activities very often. We may not have lived in poverty, but our parents didn't make enough money to offer us such leisure. Then, there are those of us that lived in extreme poverty. We didn't know what it was like to have a bed, let alone a house to live in.

At no fault of their own, our parents were trying to provide but somehow continually fell short. Perhaps they were uneducated and lacked the means that would allow them to fix our living situation. Maybe your father was abusive towards your mom or your parents were drug addicts or alcoholics.

As a society, we don't talk about the insufficiency and absence of basic resources much because we're made to believe that the deficits in our lives doesn't compare to what others experience in theirs. There will always be someone who suffers more, someone who needs more, so let's not talk about it. It's selfish; be grateful. However, there's one thing that people often don't verbalize, and it's the very thing that shapes us into adulthood. That's the child in us.

Your child self is still in you; in fact, they never left.

For people that had tough upbringings, they do everything in their power to forget those kids. Unknowingly, by doing that, we deprive ourselves of healing. Close your eyes and imagine for a minute the worst moment of your life as a child. Perhaps for you it was the moment you were sexually abused or it was the first time you saw your father hit your mom and you didn't do anything to help her or maybe it was the time you were homeless. If you were sitting next to your younger self today, what would you say? How would you interact with yourself? Would you show affection? Would you be angry?

No matter your response, understand that children shouldn't be exposed to atrocities in the first place. We all know and can agree that they should be sheltered and given the opportunity to just be a kid. But the sad truth is many kids never had a chance because of what happened in their families.

Maybe you know someone who was that kid, or perhaps you were that kid. So many adults today were robbed of their innocence, and in order to survive, they were forced to make adult decisions at a young age. Their parents were obligated to labor long hours and believed that the harder they grinded, things improved. They genuinely believed hard work was the answer; subsequently, their children were left to fend for themselves, emotionally and sometimes, physically.

In America, what is the goal of the hard work? We hear it all the time: the American Dream! Working to reach the middle class means you can have it all, right? For years, that's what we were taught. But what is the American Dream anyway? Nowadays, it seems like a faraway concept. A fantasy!

> Can you admit that you have experienced situations in your life
> that could have very well put you in the same situation your
> difficult family member is in?

The only reason you're not in that situation is because you made different decisions than they did. Maybe you found the right mate that exposed you to better living conditions: and that exposure is what enabled you to try harder; to give more; to apply yourself and fight for the things you want.

Remember this, the difficult family member going through the torments of life has a deep, dark story to tell. But society has taught them not to speak about it. Instead, what happens is a cycle of misunderstandings that drown out the reality that we truly are all the same.

WHAT IS CONTAINED IN THIS BOOK?

If you are frustrated because you believe you should be further than you are right now or have experienced rejection by your family and friends because of decisions you've made in your past or if perhaps you are simply lost and burdened by daily defeats and feel like you are running out of options to better your situation, contained in this book are answers you've been searching for. As you read through the chapters, you will see how this book can shift the trajectory of your life. You will learn that your voice means something. You will discover that with the right exposure, your relationships can be restored. You'll see that you cannot only provide for your family, but you can also find a support system that is meaningful to your future. When you finish reading this book you will know you have something to offer people and you'll be assured that what you bring to society is special. Can you imagine what that looks like?

I can, because I've lived it.

Before you read my story, know that much of what you will read here I have never told a soul.

You are the first, and writing it all down for the first time I guess is my form of therapy. I got a lot of flak for writing this book. People judged me, asking why I was doing it in the first place. Many assumed that all I wanted was attention. To be honest, this book is showing to be the best thing I could have done for myself. To let it all out.

How can I move on if I don't let it all out? How can I help others if I keep hiding who I am?

At times, it was hard to see the screen as I typed because of the tears that kept filling up my eyes, as I relived all the moments of despair and torment I experienced.

I wish I could erase the memories; in fact, I think I did a pretty good job of hiding it for thirty years.

I must confess that it has been one of the hardest things I've ever done. Finding the time to write it is hard enough; writing it is even more challenging. But neither of those is why it was difficult for me to write this book. I wrestled with exactly what to put in and what to leave out. I have children, family, great friends, I go to church, and countless others look up to me. I did not want to write a tell-all book that would expose me as not being the perfect person they might think I am. However, when I stopped thinking of myself, and put my focus on you, the reader, without knowing it, you encouraged me to write my story, warts and all.

Should you manifest what you read here, it has the potential to change your reality. Visualize what your best life looks like. Are you free from anxiety and depression? Are you free from the fear of what your future will bring? Are you confident that you have the power to better your life? Imagine a future where you're capable of providing for yourself. You know there is a way out and have learned that you can endure what life throws your way, because you found a better way to live and thrive.

You may not think so right now, but you can have this and I'm going to show you how.

2

NOBODY LIKES CHANGES

THE GOOD OLE' DAYS

My father is a preacher. From the time I was born till the age of ten life was good. Sure, I witnessed my parents struggle but my mind wasn't wrapped around negativity back then. When you were young and innocent, if you're being honest, despite your living conditions, you naturally embraced being in the moment and didn't have a care in the world. You didn't automatically think the worst when presented with a new situation.

Children are authentic, vulnerable, and not afraid to laugh. They're fascinated with things, because to them everything is new, exciting, and full of possibilities. Life is an experience, and they're captivated by it, fully engaged. For instance, how many times have you heard a child ask the question, "Why?" They'll ask it repeatedly and won't take no for an answer because they believe everything has an answer. They have a remarkable ability to indulge in joy, noticing the small but striking things in life, like a flower blooming or the way a fish moves about in an aquarium. That ability allows them to live from the heart.

Then one day, it all changes. Can you recall when it changed for you?

The clarity you had before about life somehow had become blurred.

You were more attuned to responsibilities and the difficulties of life. Worry and anxiety creeped in, got cozy, and made themselves at home in you. Suddenly, you cared about what was coming around the corner. You tried to detach yourself from the feelings of misery over growing up too fast but failed. What happened? What clicked in your mind that made you view the world differently?

When I was in the fifth grade, I would describe that time in my life being the good ole' days; it was 1991. Lenny Kravitz, in his hit song of the same name, told us, *"It ain't over till it's over."* Boy was he right. That was the same year Color Me Badd sang, *"I wanna sex you up."* Such a great song, but I was ten years old; what did I know about sex? Lol!

Teenagers were showing off their crop tops and parachute pants, watching *My Girl* with Anna Chlumsky and Macaulay Culkin, or *Boys In The Hood* with Cuba Gooding Jr. and Ice Cube.

I lived in the Sunshine State of Florida at the time, where it's warm year-round and, to top it off, I lived ten minutes from the beach. I can still feel the ocean breeze on my skin and smell the salt in the air. Man do I miss living there. I used to ride my bike around the city of Fort Lauderdale for hours every day after school and on the weekends, with not a worry in the world. It was incredible, I felt so free.

I was still so innocent then. The feeling of happiness firmly hugged me and pressed its cheek tightly against mine. I never quite understood why I felt so connected to South Florida. But writing this book is revealing to me why I crave to be there so much. That time in my life was the last time I remember feeling happy, safe, and secure. I felt an agile certainty that my future would be amazing and was eager to learn new things, especially if it meant adventurous things. I had a positive attitude and believed I could do anything and be anything. The world was full of possibilities.

WHAT CELEBRATIONS?

Although we struggled financially, my parents tried to give us everything we needed. What we needed had to take precedence over what we wanted. Birthdays weren't any different. My parents were forced to make decisions no parent should ever have to make, feeding their kids or allowing one to have a birthday party. It was the same with Christmas. We simply didn't get these celebrations, none of us did. In elementary school, the weeks leading to Christmas Day had kids bragging about what Santa was bringing them on Christmas morning. One day, I was at the mall with my mom and begged her to let me take a picture with Santa. I believed with everything in my heart that this man was the Santa the kids talked about at school. I was so excited!

Finally, I was meeting Santa, the one person that had the power to bring me what I wanted for Christmas that year, a new bike. We stood in line, and I watched the kids with huge smiles on their faces. Their eyes, like mine, glowed with expectation. Finally, it was my turn. I headed down the long path, walking on red carpet. When I got to the front, I immediately sat on his lap, and then he said to me,

"Hi what's your name?" I eagerly replied, "Priscilla." He asked, "Priscilla, what do you want for Christmas this year?" I said, "I want a new bike." Then he said, "Oh, wow, that's a great gift for a girl your age. Priscilla, this year you will get a new bike." I left the mall that day feeling like I was walking on clouds. Now I understood what the kids at school felt like; it was incredible. The next couple of weeks I shared the excitement with my friends when we talked about what we all were getting for Christmas.

It was the same year *National Lampoon's Christmas Vacation* was released. That was such a good movie, and I watched it over and over as I waited for Christmas Day to arrive. In the movie, Clark Griswold's family all come to his house to celebrate Christmas together. I found it captivating that each person came bearing gifts to put under the tree. I knew that my extended family couldn't simply come over; they were all left behind in Brazil. But if they could come over, I was positive they'd come bearing gifts too.

I took it upon myself to substitute their gifts by wrapping items I found lying around the house. Then I filled the ground around the Christmas tree and called them presents. When Christmas Eve arrived, I was thrilled. I couldn't control my excitement when I pictured the way my new bike looked. I went to bed early and expectedly waited to fall asleep. Knowing that the next day I was getting the best present ever, I woke up early. My parents were still sleeping, and I ran to the living room.

To my surprise, all I saw under the tree were the presents I wrapped. I looked all over the house and found nothing else. I was heartbroken. *Where is my bike?* I ran to my parent's room, "Mom, Dad! Where is my bike?" They replied, "Bike?" Rubbing their eyes as they laughed. "What bike? We didn't buy you a bike" *Surely, they were confused too*, I thought. "No!" I said, "the bike Santa brought me. Where is it?" Their laughter grew even louder, and then I started to cry. "Why are you laughing?" I asked.

I told them that at the mall, when I sat on Santa's lap, I asked him for a new bike. And he told me I would get one for Christmas. It took them a minute to get their composure, then they told me, "There's no such thing as Santa, Priscilla. We are Santa, and we can't afford to buy you a new bike. If we buy you a bike, no one eats" Ah! The devastation. *That man lied to me? How could someone be so cruel? He told me I was getting the bike I always wanted. And now my parents are telling me there's no such thing as Santa? Whose lap did I sit on then?* By now, you're probably thinking why my parents would crush my spirit like that on Christmas Day.

Why be so brash? It's hard to be that brutally honest with your kids. But before you judge them, put yourself in their shoes. How do you explain to your child that you can't afford to buy them anything more than the clothes they have on their backs and the food they need to eat to survive? What's harsher, telling the truth or lying to them? What would you have said to soften the blow?

Sure, maybe they didn't have to laugh. But what I was asking for was so far-fetched to them. Think about it for a minute. If they bought me a bike, which probably costed $120 or so back then, no one in my family would have food to eat for the week. I may have been immature and naïve as a kid, but I knew struggle when I saw it. I recognized the difference in the lifestyles my friends lived compared to mine. In the end I accepted that I wasn't getting a bike that year. I was still upset by the whole ordeal but I understood the position may parents were in.

WHAT HAPPENED?

My family lived in a blue two-story house. The floors weren't attached like a normal two-story house so the only way to get to the second floor was from an exterior staircase located on the side of the building. The landlord lived on the top floor. By the time I was eight, my sister Soraya and I were the only two girls living with my parents and my three brothers. My two older sisters, Eklesia and Layla, were married and had families of their own.

In most of the stories you will read about in this book, you'll find me reference my sister Soraya. She and I were inseparable, as she is almost a year older than me. In fact, we are the same age for four days. My sister and me shared a small room, big enough to fit a bunk bed and a small dresser.

One Saturday morning, I was in my room, sitting on my bed and eating a bowl of cereal. I was beginning to plan out the day in my head. I was certain, like always, that ice cream and video games would be in my future that day. Except minutes later, my mom called us into the living room because my dad had an announcement to make. I walked across the hardwood floor holding the cereal bowl in my hand and sat down on the edge of our green couch in the living room. My mom turned off the TV, and my dad began to speak. I soon heard the words, "We're moving to a town called Albuquerque."

My mind went completely blank, and I can't remember anything else my parents said that morning. But what I can remember was feeling angry. I was so annoyed by the news and had never been so mad, irritated, and livid like the way I felt that day. I loved Florida. I loved living near the beach. Why would we leave such a beautiful place? At the time, my parents didn't say much about where we were going, other than there were mountains there. That made me a little curious because I never seen mountains before. But still!

It was the middle of my summer vacation. I didn't say bye to any of my friends because I never thought in a million years that the last day of school would be the last time I'd see them. I didn't have anyone's phone number. Cell phones weren't a thing yet, and social media, ha, that certainly didn't exist. There was no way I could reach out to my friends and tell them they would never see me again, all because my parents decided to move.

For weeks we packed up everything we could and stuffed it in an open trailer bed my dad attached to his brown 1980 Pontiac Bonneville. My parents couldn't afford a U-Haul, so we had to make multiple trips driving from South Florida to Albuquerque.

The first trip back, my dad got pulled over. The empty trailer was swaying back and forth on the highway, making my dad look like he was driving drunk. I've never seen my dad drunk. Ever! Luckily, the officer let us go with a warning. I supposed it was obvious my dad wasn't drunk; he was just tired. Weeks later, there we were driving again; it was round two, driving back to Albuquerque with more stuff. This time, my dad had no money. Obviously during the multiple trips back and forth my dad couldn't work. My mom was a stay-at-home mom. Most of my life my father was the sole provider for our family, so you can imagine the difficulty and stress we all faced during this move. Many times, we'd go hours without having any food to eat. Things got so bad the second trip that my sister and I tried to make light of the situation by playing travel games in the back seat of the car.

Eventually, the hunger got the best of us. Hangry isn't the word to describe what we were feeling. Before the weakness and fatigue kicked in, we fought. A lot. We knew we'd get in trouble so, as to not disturb my dad, we quietly dug our nails into each other's arms as we intently made eye contact. Whoever let go first lost. After the fighting and bickering came the worst part. I've never been so famished. Have you ever waited too long to eat that you got stomachaches? There's a point where your stomach stops growling, and you're simply downright weak. I sensed myself fading, many times. A good meal was all I wanted. Not knowing when that would happen was terrifying to say the least.

Finally, my dad came across some food. Don't ask me how; I was so lethargic I can't remember the details. Maybe it was an answered prayer. But don't get your hopes up; it's not what you're thinking. It wasn't the food I was hoping for either. What was it, you ask? Bread and oranges. There was so much of it, it filled up the trunk. For three days, that's all we ate.

QUESTION EVERYTHING

I learned quickly after moving to Albuquerque that life was not all it was cracked out to be there. The positive attitude I once had disappeared. The belief that I could do anything and be anything, faded fast. The world wasn't full of possibilities anymore. Moving from a beautiful oceanside city to a dry, brown, and dead-looking town in the desert was dreadful. The summer of 1991 was supposed to be the best one yet. I graduated from elementary school and was ready to start middle school with my friends.

Instead, it turned into the summer where I became the girl in the hood. Literally! Don't believe me? A couple of months into living in Albuquerque, I witnessed a drive-by shooting.

There I was, standing in front of a locally owned grocery store, staring at the lifeless body of a teenage boy lying on the concrete. Before this, I didn't know anything about gangs or guns, let alone violence and death. I was traumatized. No child should grow up seeing things like that. I quivered in disbelief, stunned and speechless by what was unfolding in front of my eyes. While the police were doing their investigation, the boy laid there for what felt like a lifetime. It's as if time slowed down, long enough for the image to be seared into my mind. Everything was moving in slow motion, like a scene from a thriller.

What was even more astonishing was I didn't see anyone crying for the kid lying dead on the ground. I wondered why. Why was no one frightened, alarmed, or even upset by what just happened? Did no one care? Where the hell was I? What kind of place was I living in?

That was the moment in my life when I began to question everything.

Everything! Why was this happening? Why would my family move here? Did they not see what type of place it was? In fact, why was I even born into this family? Did God make a mistake? There's no way He wanted this for us.

For me.

I couldn't believe God intentionally brought me into this world to live like that, to see things like that. I began questioning my very existence. Why was I born at all? For the first time I didn't feel seen or heard by anyone. My voice meant nothing, and the things happening around me made no sense. Don't get me wrong; I love my family. But why the hell would we come to this place? Albuquerque, New Mexico?

To me, it was a horrific place to raise a family. Was I purposely being set up to fail? It sure felt like it. I didn't have a support system or anyone that I could trust or talk to. I didn't talk to my parents about the shooting. I was so mad at them for making us move that frankly, I didn't want to hear anything they had to say. All I knew at the time was that my dad moved us to Albuquerque because he felt he had a calling to start a church there. At the age of ten, I was already enslaved by daily burdens like anxiety and depression, struggling with the fear of what the future held for me. My world was falling apart! I was surrounded by gangs and violence.

After months of living in fear, I felt useless, incapable, and unworthy. There was no way out, and I had no power to change my environment. So, I numbed myself to any sense of restraint, accountability, or guilt for the new place we called home. Nobody else cared, so why should I?

I began ignoring the desperation to escape and accepted my new reality. I hated everything about my life, and I didn't want to hear excuses of why we came to this God-forsaken town. There was not one thing anyone can tell me that would justify my parents' decision, so I stretched my arms out wide, closed my eyes, leaned forward, and slowly free-fell into a deep, dark chasm of recklessness.

The next eight years, I was convinced that I would become a statistic.

Feeling like that influenced my behavior. I stopped caring. About everything, I opened myself up to the idea of hanging out with gangsters. My curiosity gripped their attention, and they began to groom me. Eventually, I started to believe that one day I'd end up like that teenage boy. Lifeless. Shot dead by the people he wished he could run away from. He was trapped too, just like me. His only way out was death because he was stuck in his environment: hopeless, trapped, and worthless, with nowhere else to go. He had no means that could shift the trajectory of his life. Like me, he didn't get to choose his family or where he lived. So, I thought, what's the use? Since I don't have many years of life left anyway, I might as well have fun.

Be rebellious. Be uncontrollable. Be wild.

3

I AM WHO I AM

LITTLE DID I KNOW

I was having fun alright. I had easy access to any drug I could get my hands on and surrounded myself with the worst type of people you might imagine. You name it.

- Dangerous
- Spiteful
- Mean
- Cruel
- Manipulative
- Ghetto
- Drug-addicted
- Reckless
- Irresponsible
- Disrespectful, and the list goes on…

I'm a preacher's kid, so if hanging out with those people meant making my parents suffer, I took pleasure in doing it. Every time I thought about Florida, I became more and more aggravated by their decision. But little did I know that by acting like that, I exposed myself to the cruelest life lessons you could conceive.

FAMILY CULTURE

Why do you suppose kids act this way? By now, you can agree that childhood experiences influence the adults we become. For example, the foundation of our home life becomes the foundation that the rest of our lives are built on. If this foundation is fractured, the emotional wounds and hurts that come from it have an incredible impact on the makeup of our adult lives.

Every single one of us has a story. Like it or not, we each walk out our childhood stories in everything we do. As adults, over time, we learn to fill our stories with the memories we had of our childhoods.

Some of us remember the way our parents argued or perhaps how our siblings mistreated us or how our early teen years were hell. It's our memories that underline our stories, then our stories underline our thoughts, and those thoughts are what develop the why behind who we become.

Likewise, birth order has an impact on our story and how we carry that into adulthood. My birth order is last, the baby of seven children.

It's always the youngest child that gets categorized as the spoiled brat. The stereotype is that they got so much attention that it led them to feeling entitled as an adult. Entitled adults get upset when they don't get their way, which could lead to frustration and fear. I wouldn't say I was spoiled per se. Yes, my mom stepped in and did everything for me, like cleaning my room, folding my clothes, and making me a plate at dinner time. Regardless, however, we were all poor, extremely poor, and there's no way, to me anyway, that I could be defined as being spoiled.

My entire family struggled. A lot. What my mom did for me didn't make me an entitled adult that gets upset when I don't get my way, and it sure didn't lead to me getting depressed or having anxiety. In fact, what my mom did for me was genuine. For both me and my sister Soraya, while living in Albuquerque, she softened the blow of poverty for us.

My parents were born and raised in Brazil. The bout of severe poverty with two young girls living at home, in fact, was round two for my mom. Round one happened in Brazil with my two older sisters' Layla and Eklesia. They're the ones I mentioned earlier who had moved out already and had families of their own. Looking back, I see how my mom tried her best to change our perspective because she had no other choice. She was a stay-at-home mom for most of her life. During my early teen years, she got a job washing sheets and towels at the Hyatt nearby so she could provide my sister and me with things like snacks for school, a good breakfast, pads and tampons, make-up, clothes, and new underwear. All the things were what a pre-teen girl needed in order to enter womanhood less afraid from living an impoverished lifestyle.

My family culture growing up fell short of a fulfilled American Dream, that's for sure. But I was taught to work hard, be honest, have integrity, and to commit myself to always trying my best.

I'M NOT HIDING ANYMORE

At the risk of being embarrassed and humiliated, you are holding the truest account of my life. Though it has been painful, I have decided to let everything out—the good, the bad, the ugly, and even the private ugly things I thought I'd never tell a soul. I risked showing you this because my motive is to motivate and encourage you to not hide who you are like I did. I have been blessed to have found inspiration from others, and now I'm attempting to bring some of that to your life. I believe that you are a blessing and can be a blessing to others no matter what your life looked like. I believe you have it in you and believe you have the vision and the will to live the life your Creator designed especially for you.

CREED

What is a creed? According to the New Oxford American Dictionary, creed is:

"a set of fundamental beliefs, a guiding principle[1]."

Despite me and my siblings' shortcomings and rebellious moments, as early as I can remember, because of my parents, we were in tune with our spirituality. In fact, so much of my story you will find has a spiritual connotation to it.

I didn't do that on purpose; it's just who I am. My life experiences somehow have always tied into my creed. And it wasn't subtle either: it was loud, brash, and in your face. There was no denying it. You'll see what I mean as you read on. My parents were strict, especially when it came to doing activities with friends. Whenever we dared to ask, the answer was most often a resounding no.

- No, you can't spend the night at your friend's house.
- No, you can't go to the movies.
- No, you can't watch that show.
- No, you can't listen to that song.

Despite my family's creed, I was a terrible kid. I didn't listen, at all. Rebellion doesn't even begin to describe how much of a jerk I was to my parents.

For years, I tried to run away from my upbringing as a Christian.

But no matter how much I tried to run, I couldn't get away from my faith. The conditions I was exposed to rings true to me still to this day. Believe me when I say that many stories will appear unusual to you, perhaps even strange. But all of them are as true as it gets. I left out no details. And each of them best describes how my memories fill in the story from a childhood that formed the adult I am today.

4
WHO ARE WE?

MY PARENTS

My family is from São Paulo, Brazil. My parents met each other at the local church they attended. My father, Alberto, was a good-looking young man; my mom, Maria, was beautiful! Of course. She told me my dad was popular with the ladies at church, but not in the way you might think. The girls at church tried hard to get his attention because they sensed he was an ambitious man not afraid to take risks. People sometimes attribute Christianity to being a dull way to live. So, for the ladies back then, spontaneity, you can imagine, was naturally attractive.

In their teens, my parents both made a promise to themselves that they would one day marry someone who lived a disciplined, devout Christian lifestyle. They each wanted a person that took pride in putting God first in all they did. This promise is what ultimately brought them together. My mom was dating someone else the first time she met my dad, except her boyfriend was not a Christian. The way my mom tells the story is she broke up with her boyfriend because he was not aligning with the promise, she made to herself.

After the breakup, she started to pay more attention to my dad. The interest turned into a massive crush, except at first, my dad wouldn't give her the time of day. This sounds eerily like the story of how I met my husband, but I'll fill you in on that later.

What's fascinating is knowing that what attracted my dad to my mom was her unrelenting faith in Christ.

She had discernment and understood the power of prayer, even at a young age. She was an intercessor, and still is today. She had all the attributes my dad wanted since the age of eighteen, but that wasn't all. She was trustworthy, someone he knew would take care of the home, be faithful to him, and who possessed a selfless attitude. He knew that he was doing right by choosing my mom as a wife. In fact, I doubt my mom has ever sinned a day in her life.

And I'm not exaggerating. Anyone who knows my mother would agree 1000% and would tell you I'm telling the truth. After three years or so of dating, my dad proposed. The eve of their wedding day, my mom's ex-boyfriend showed up at her doorstep. She was astonished. After all that time, the guy heard about her engagement and decided to show up the days before her wedding. The nerve!

He traveled far just to tell her that he turned his life around and was finally the man she promised herself she would one day marry. She couldn't believe what she was hearing. Turned out, he had become a successful restaurant owner; even my grandparents gave her the green light to choose who she wanted to be with because to them they were both good choices. She knew, from a financial perspective, her ex had the means to provide for her and for their future children. Plus, he was her first love, the love of her life. She was certain they'd have a great life together. But nonetheless, as difficult as it was for her, she told the one man she waited for that he was too late.

Caught between her past love and her new love, my mom displayed a rare level of commitment. She loved my dad; he was the man she prayed for her whole life. And who's to say that her ex-boyfriend wouldn't one day decide he didn't want to be a Christian anymore. It happens to a lot of people. My mom decided to stay with the man that put God first, the man she knew would provide a godly home for her children and not the man that chose God when he realized he was losing the girl. The next ten years of my parents' life together, my mother birthed seven children and miscarried two. Today my parents have been married fifty-three years and are still going strong.

WHY SEVEN CHILDREN?

I often wondered where the desire for so many children came from. Turns out my mom only wanted two, but my dad was determined to have seven. The number seven, in the Bible, symbolizes completion or perfection. Growing up, my dad told us a story about a near-death experience he had when he was eighteen years old. It was that experience that changed the way he thought about his future family.

As a teenager, my dad dreamed of making a difference in people's lives. He believed it was his purpose and was convinced he could fulfill it by becoming a pastor. The dream became his passion. The passion was so intense that he deprived himself of having fun with his friends because he feared doing that would hurt his focus.

In 1962 one evening, while holding a Bible in his right hand, my dad was walking to church. He was on a path he traveled on dozens of times before. There was a bridge he had to cross to get into town, and that evening, as he was approaching the bridge, a strange man advanced toward him. It was an awkward moment because my dad had never seen the man before. Nonetheless, the man got close to his face, then signaled with his eyes for my dad to look down. That's when my dad saw the knife. The sharp end was touching my dad's stomach. What was interesting was that the man said he had no intention of robbing my dad. All he said was he wanted to stab him and leave him for dead on the sidewalk. Who says that!?!

The only explanation for that type of behavior is that of pure evil. And sure enough, my dad sensed there was a malicious manifestation that was encircling the man, the type of presence that sends chills down your spine. It was an evil so cruel that the only way to expel it is to pray. Fortunately, my dad knew immediately what he was dealing with, so he looked into the man's eyes. He forcefully stared at him, and said, "I know who you are. And you know you have no authority over my life."

The man gave him a dirty look back and said,

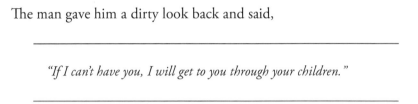

"If I can't have you, I will get to you through your children."

Then, nonchalantly, he put the knife down and walked away.

That was the day, my dad explained, he knew that in order to fulfill his purpose, he had to make difficult decisions to protect his children. So, he made it a priority to marry someone who not only knew God intimately, but who had an unrelenting faith in Christ. Someone who was discerning and understood the power of prayer—he wanted an intercessor for his children. And that's my mom.

MY FAMILY'S LINEAGE

My oldest sister Eklesia took a 23 *and me* DNA test not too long ago, and I thought it would be fun to share it here with you. This is what we discovered: my family is:

- 66% European
- 22% Sub-Saharan African
- 10% East Asian and Indigenous American and,
- 2% Western Asian and North African.

It's safe to say my family is a melting pot of awe-inspiring ethnicities and explains the vast variety of races in my family. I have aunts, uncles, and cousins who are blonde with blue eyes, Asian, Black and everything in between. My mom's father was gorgeous. He was a Black man with the bluest eyes you'd ever see. I don't remember much about my grandparents. But what I can remember I'll share.

MY GRANDPARENTS

My dad was very much a mama's boy. His dad left when he was young, so he was raised by my grandmother. I can only imagine how hard that must have been for my grandmother, being a single mom in the 1940s. She raised six children, five daughters and one son, by herself. What's sad is the only memory I have of my grandmother on my dad's side was the day he found out she passed away; it was shortly after we moved to the States. She begged my dad not to leave Brazil, but he was determined to give his family a better future, I was six years old. He couldn't afford to bring my grandmother, so he was obligated to leave without her.

The way he tells it is, she died of a broken heart.

Can you imagine!?! The guilt he must have felt for leaving her. Wow! Writing this for the first time is heartbreaking. It makes me sad knowing he had to live through that for us.

My mother grew up in a farm with both her parents in the home. Opposite of my dad, she was the only girl and had five brothers. The farm was deep in the woods, far away from the city. I guess it's safe to say they lived in the Amazon. My mom's dad was a devout Christian and extremely strict. She told us stories of how he'd wake up the entire family at 5:00 a.m. to have a church service in the living room. They read Scripture, sang songs, and ended with a short sermon given by her father. No one was allowed to fall asleep; she said the kids all struggled to stay awake. If they fell asleep, well, you can assume what came next. Hint: it rhymes with banking.

For my mom's parents, I have a few more memories. I wish I had more, but I do remember going to their house. My grandfather loved to make a Brazilian candy called cocada. It's a sweet coconut bar, made with a lot of melted sugar and fresh coconut shavings. It tasted so good. My grandfather snuck us in the kitchen to give us some while they were super soft and chewy, before they dried. Yum!

In the farm, there were dozens of chickens. If you've ever been to Hawaii, you will know what wild chickens look like running around. I don't remember seeing chicken coops though, just chickens, everywhere.

As a child I didn't think about why suddenly only one chicken was running around inside the kitchen. As soon as the chicken was trapped, my grandmother yelled for my mom to take the kids away. One time, as I left the room, I turned a corner that led into the living room. I heard a loud WHACK, followed by a loud screeching sound. We weren't allowed back in the kitchen until the bird was clean, defeathered, and ready to cook.

My grandparents on either side didn't have the means to deliver an abundance of material or financial resources to my parents and their siblings. But their determination was an encouragement to everyone around them. They were driven and committed to raising their kids to the best of their abilities. Their modesty, passion for family, and influence they handed down to my parents are priceless. I'm thankful for the courage and purpose they passed down, which then later passed on to me. And now I can pass on the same thing to my children.

GROWING UP

Between the ages of 6 and 9, in church, as a pastor's kid, life brought its own share of challenges. Despite those challenges I was still naïve, immature, and innocent. The only thing I was thinking about then was recess and playing with my friends after school. I remember being laughed at because I didn't speak English very well and my clothes were all hand me downs. I didn't quite recognize that bullying was wrong, but assumed kids were cruel because I was the new kid.

I never correlated my feeling like a subordinate or inferior to others in school as something bad. I honestly expected to feel that way because I wasn't from the United States. Additionally, I was confined to a certain way of thinking; surrounded by judging eyes was normal being a pastor's kid. So, when I found myself feeling distressed or trapped in school, I accepted it. But when I turned ten, things changed. I was learning more about myself, what I liked and disliked. For the first time, I felt anxiety and guilt over wanting to do things like sneaking in magazine pages and hiding it in my Bible while my dad was preaching in church.

Whenever I told my friends I was a pastor's kid, they assumed right away that I was a goody-two- shoes. The expectation of the type of person I was expected to be made life miserable. Eventually everyone knew me as a pastor's kid and expected me to behave that way.

There was constant pressure of not being permitted to make mistakes, even outside of church, the heaviness I felt as a kid living with that type of burden.

I'd become afraid of what people would say if I expressed struggles or shared battles. To them, I didn't, and shouldn't, have struggles.

And battles? What battles? Christians don't deal with that! Right? God loves them so much that they don't have any problems.

There were numerous times I thought church was tedious. But sharing that with anyone would be horrific. I dreaded the fear of being condemned for thinking like that, so I hid it. I believe the reason I didn't collapse under all that pressure was because of my upbringing. It's an oxymoron but it's true. Turns out, the one thing that put so much pressure on me to live a holy life was the very thing that helped me through the anxiety of living under that much pressure. I was taught that whenever I felt fear, panic, worry, or pain, I should lean on God; to pray through it and ask Jesus to bring me peace; and to have faith that everything was going to be alright.

IMMIGRANT

I wish I could sit here today and tell you that everything was alright, but I can't. Countless times, things were not alright. As an immigrant moving to the United States, life was extremely difficult. Think about it for a minute. Parents who want to provide a better life for their families give up everything to make that happen. But after they make the move, they're in a strange land. They don't know the language. They don't know the culture. They don't understand the systems or the politics. They're just desperate to provide for their families.

In America, we see millions of people just like my parents who have courageously journeyed the roads less traveled, all in the name of a better future. Immigrants are hard workers and entrepreneurial. They possess a will to take risks that most Americans can't understand and will tolerate inconvenience for the slim chance of changing their circumstances.

To be honest, I believe that when given the right resources and support, immigrants will always give back to their communities in a heartfelt and meaningful way. They're not afraid to share their knowledge and experiences to better others. Isn't that the way we should all be? The thing is, humans are designed to work and provide; that is how we thrive in society.

Think about it: when have you seen a toddler accomplish something as simple as getting on a chair and get sad or upset because someone else didn't do it for them? The opposite happens. They're proud. They understand that what they just experienced is what accomplishment feels like. What happens after that? Their confidence goes through the roof, and they smile as they do that same thing repeatedly.

We are created for success.

I agree that helping immigrants get on their feet is important. Heck, I wish my parents accepted the help when we first moved to the States. But they refused it because they didn't want handouts. They believed that people should work for the things they have. There is something to be said about giving people so much that they forget what it feels like to accomplish things on their own. I believe help should be offered in the form of resources that will build a population, not keep them dependent.

I've read books on poverty, and one thing I've learned is that when you strip the ability of a population to provide for themselves, you inadvertently keep that population poor, in despair, and unable to contribute at levels that they know they can. They become hopeless and are reminded every day that they can't provide for their families on their own. They're stuck and stripped of the satisfying feeling accomplishment brings.

My parents were fearless; they had to be.

They endured so much suffering and discomfort to provide for us, but their ability to remain faithful to the process was an epic display of their character.

In the next few chapters, I will be sharing the most vulnerable parts of my life growing up. And I want to make this crystal clear . . . As you read on, the last thing I want you to consider is that my parents didn't try. They did try. Every day, they tried.

The life of an immigrant is no walk in the park. We had nothing! We were isolated and alone. We were confined to a level of distress many people in this country could not endure. My parents are survivors. They are fighters; they are entrepreneurs; they are visionaries; and they're my heroes.

5

AN IMMIGRANT'S JOURNEY

WHAT BROUGHT US TO THE UNITED STATES?

For years, I shared the story of what made my parents move to Albuquerque, New Mexico. It wasn't until just days ago, literally, I found out I had it all wrong. I was shocked to learn that Albuquerque was the reason we came to the United States in the first place. I can't believe I've lived in the U.S. for thirty-five years and didn't know this.

I was out to dinner with my oldest sister, Eklesia and my three kids. That night, my kids happen to ask my sister how we came to the States, and that's when we learned the details. The kids were as surprised as I was. You can imagine the look on my face, hearing the true account for the first time in my life. Turns out years before I was born, while still living in Brazil, my father had a dream.

Ok! Hold on. Before I continue, this slice of the story is not for everyone.

In fact, it sounds a little crazy, which explains why the version I was told when I was younger was different. Many of you won't understand it, and that's okay. But it's the truth, and I am going to tell it anyway. For those of you that have awareness of growing up in a Christian home, my father had a vision. I say vision because he was awake when this happened. But for the sake of those of you who are not familiar with visions, we'll stick to, "Well . . . He had a dream."

The way my sister tells it is like this: "He was transported from his body into an unknown place." I'm not going to begin to pretend I know how visions work, let alone how our bodies, minds, souls, and consciousness are aligned, but I assume perhaps his conscience departed from his body. Who knows!?!

"He was walking the streets of this place, and he heard a different language being spoken. He could tell right away it was not Portuguese. As he walked, he thought to himself, *How am I going to ask someone where I am?* He didn't remember how he figured it out, but he came up to a person on the street and asked them where he was, and the person said, "You're in Albuquerque." Then he snapped out of it."

Eklesia said this happened three years before I was born, and eight years before we moved to the United States. Eklesia was seven. Just wait, it gets more interesting.

"Shortly after the vision, Dad came home with a huge map. He taped the map to a wall in our house and started looking for Albuquerque. He first looked all over Brazil, and . . . Nothing! He kept going up, going up, and going up until he got to the U.S. He searched until finally he found New Mexico. And there it was! The city called Albuquerque. He looked to Mom, and said, "That's where we're going." For the next three years, he kept saying it repeatedly. "That's where we're going. That's where we're going." Almost as if he was trying to convince himself that it was a good idea.

As my sister is telling me this story, my brain is exploding. For decades, I wondered why Albuquerque. Now I'm convinced that there is a reason I was brought to this city. And I'm determined to figure out what my purpose is here. She continued:

"For three years, Dad was talking about coming to Albuquerque, so he began praying about it. Asking God to show him how he was going to get here. Then one day, while at our church in Osasco, Brazil, remember he's the pastor, he turned to the congregation and said, 'It's time for me to go.'"

Eklesia remembers seeing everyone's faces in the congregation as they asked my dad, "Go? What do you mean? Where are you going?" And he tells them, "Albuquerque."

"In a few short days, he moved the family out of Osasco, back to the house we used to live in, next door to Grandma's house. From that point, it took two more years for him to gather the money and get his papers in order. It wasn't until then that he came to the United States for the first time. He lived here for three years.

Meanwhile, Mom stayed in Brazil, raising seven kids on her own. It was hell living over there without Dad.

Without a husband. A lot of people in the church ridiculed Mom for that, asking why her husband just left her there with all those kids. Mom went through hell! When he finally came back to Brazil, he said, 'Alright! Everybody, it's time to go.' He had green cards for everyone. We took a bus to Rio De Janeiro, Brazil to sit in front of a consulate employee.

"When we got there, we all went into a small room. The man, sitting in his chair, leaned back and crossed his arms. He just stared at us for a while. Dad was looking back at the guy, as he sat there with seven kids and his wife. The man started to shake his head back and forth. For a minute, he didn't know what to say. He was astonished. When he finally opened his mouth, he said, 'Are you telling me you're going to go to the United States of America with all these children, and no money?'

"Dad, said, 'yup!' 'How much money do you have?' the man asked. Dad showed him what he had in his hand and says, 'This much.' Then the man said, 'And you got green cards for all of them, I can see. And you have all the papers in order?' Dad said, 'Absolutely!' Then the man replied, 'Holy Jesus!'

"Stamp, stamp, stamp, stamp, stamp, stamp, stamp, and stamp! He stamped each of our paperwork and said, 'There you go!'

My sister recalled sitting in front of the man, just staring at him in disbelief; she was fifteen years old. My kids interrupted and asked my sister how they got everything they owned to the United States. Heck I was wondering the same thing, to be honest. I never considered her response though. I was six years old when this happened and don't remember any of it.

"There was nothing to pack," she said.

"We left everything! We came here with only the clothes on our backs. I don't even remember bringing a toothbrush. I was wearing a black dress. I had a little, cloth backpack that I put a few things in. And that was it! I was devastated! I wanted to run away! But there was no escaping."

As I was hearing this story for the first time, I was in utter shock and in complete disbelief. The only reason we went to Florida first was because the people there were the first contacts my father made in the U.S. He didn't know anyone in Albuquerque yet. So, while we lived in South Florida, he was establishing contacts in Albuquerque, New Mexico before finally moving. Seriously?

I'm forty-one years old. Everything I knew about my life growing up just blew up in my face. All the hate I stockpiled for moving to Albuquerque, and you mean to tell me that Albuquerque was the destination all along? Ahh!!! As we all sat there, in the restaurant, my kids and me were speechless. Then my sister decided to drop another bomb.

She said, "Here's the thing though. Do you know how and when he made the decision that one day he would move to America?" I replied, "Heck no!"

"He was fifteen years old. He was in a movie theater, watching a movie. A western movie.

And I remember him telling us, while he was looking at the screen, he told his friends, this movie is made in a desert somewhere in America, 'I'm gonna go to America one day.' His friends started laughing at him, saying, 'Yea sure you will.'"

Then Eklesia said, "I don't remember which movie it was, but I would bet anything that it was filmed in Albuquerque. It took Dad how long, from when he was fifteen until he got here? Twenty-six years."

I've always wondered where I get the determination to not settle until I do what's in my head. After hearing this story, now I know. I'm just like my dad. All the ridicule he got from family and friends. Calling him crazy, making fun of him because he didn't have any money. Now I understand why my dad used to tell me, "God doesn't call the prepared; He prepares the called." It makes total sense. Most people would say the stars aligned perfectly for all of us to get here. I say God made that decision and gave my dad the courage to walk it out.

IN MY FAMILY, PRAYER IS EVERYTHING

While my father was in America, you remember, my mom was left behind in Brazil for three years taking care of seven kids by herself. By the time I was five years old, I understood what prayer was, and was taught by my mom that when you pray, you must do it with an expectant heart. With faith. Not faith in the way you may be thinking. It's faith, like your prayer has already been answered and what you're asking for has already happened. Praying like that is easier said than done. Considering the fact that when we pray, it's because we're asking for something we don't have. It's difficult to ask for something in prayer and speak as if you already have what you're asking for. My mom lived this out in front of me every day of my life.

After dinner one night, my mom was crying quietly in her room. I heard my mom cry repeatedly during the three years my dad was gone.

But that evening, my curiosity peaked, and I finally drew up the nerve to ask her why she was crying.

It was dark in my room but I could hear her in her bedroom across the hallway. Holding my hands out, so I didn't trip on anything, I started to slowly walk towards the hallway. When I reached my door, I opened it and walked over to her room.

Her bedroom door was open, and her back was to me as she was kneeling on the floor. I stood at the doorway for a while, attempting to hear what she was saying. I heard her praying for God to bring us food because she knew the meal we just ate was the last meal we had. Her cry was silent. It was the kind of cry that you have when you want to cry in private, but the anguish is so much that you blurt out groans you didn't know you had in you. Finally, I found the nerve, and I walked up behind her. Quietly, I asked, "Mom, why are you crying?" She turned to me, wiping the tears off her cheek. She then smiled and said, "it's okay. I'm okay. God always provides. Remember that when you get older."

Then, like so many other times after that night, there would be a knock at the door. No one to be seen. Yet there it was, bags upon bags of groceries. My mom knew that when she cried out to God, He heard every single word and wiped every tear off her face. As my mom began to bring in the groceries, with her beautiful singing voice, she sang, "Praise the Lord. Hallelujah, Glory to God!" Then she turned to us and said, "You see, kids, when you earnestly pray for God to show up, He always does."

Today, I give credit to my parents for how they raised me. My whole life, they modeled godly behavior and what it looked like to have a good attitude despite our circumstances. They taught me to have faith and know that no matter what people say, if you are called to a purpose in life, God will see you through it. After all, God doesn't call the prepared; God prepares the called.

6

HOMELESSNESS HITS HOME

CULTURE SHOCK

As you learned in the previous chapters, my introduction to living in Albuquerque was not a good one. Well, the first day of middle school wasn't any different. In homeroom, a boy in my class offered me weed. I had no idea what it was; to be honest, I thought it was tea. I thought, *Where am I? People eat tea leaves here?* Albuquerque was such a culture shock for me from living in Florida that I assumed it was normal to eat dry tea. So, I ate it. The boy looked at me like I was nuts. Apparently, I wasn't supposed to eat it, he said I was supposed to smoke it. Within minutes, my head felt fuzzy, and I never experienced that before. I thought I was going crazy.

Oh wait, the story gets better.

The school I went to was close to our house. The town was small, so groups of kids walked home together after school. A girl I met during lunch saw me walking home and asked me if I wanted to go to her house. I thought about it for a minute and knew my parents would say no, so instead of asking, I figured, *Why not? I'm living here now so I might as well make some friends.* Regrettably, while I was sitting in her living room watching TV with her and her dad, her dad told me to pick up a roach from the ash tray that was on the coffee table. "WHAT!?!" I screamed. I expected to see a cockroach.

I was mortified when he started laughing at me and thought, *Seriously, what is he talking about? Am I stupid? Why is he laughing at me?* Embarrassed, I asked him what he was talking about. He told me that a roach is another word for a joint. He explained that a joint was something you smoked to help you "feel better." Then he told me to smoke it. That was the first time I got high; I was eleven years old. The experience was not pleasant, at all.

In fact, I hated the way I felt. I got paranoid and was scared for my life. I begged my new friend to take me home, and she laughed at me. I ran to the living room and begged her dad to take me home, and he laughed too. What the HELL! I kept asking myself, "What is wrong with these people?" I was convinced they were going to kill me, and my parents would never see me again. And of course, that made me even more suspicious that I got more and more skeptical of their intentions with me. Their laugh sounded cynical; it was disgusting.

I completely lost track of time and couldn't remember how long it had been since smoking the joint. Then the girl pulled out a pack of Virginia Slims cigarettes and started smoking it. How can a father allow his middle-schooler to live like that? All of it was foreign to me. I felt stuck in an environment that I knew was bad. Everything in my being knew it was a debauched situation, but I was jammed and wedged in so far that I did whatever they told me to do. Nevertheless, by the end of my sixth-grade year, I was addicted to the lifestyle. I became a heavy cigarette smoker, an avid weed smoker, and well on the way to becoming an alcoholic too.

My parents had no idea what was going on with me. They were busy with their full-time ministry. Just being around them made me dread the lifestyle I was living behind their backs. Despite the horror, fear, and regret, I felt so trapped in my addiction that I hid it and hid it well. I had to. However, what happened next did not help my situation one bit.

MY PRAYER WARRIOR

One year had passed, when one night, I was partying at a friend's house. Everyone was drinking, rolling blunts, and trying drugs like LSD, speed, and cocaine.

Drinking, chain-smoking cigarettes, and smoking blunts wasn't new to me, but heavier drugs were.

A guy at the party was passing out Sweet Tart candies laced with LSD. Dozens of kids at this party were sucking on the candies and tripping out like crazy. When he got to me, he asked if I wanted one and of course, without hesitation, I jumped at the opportunity.

It was my first-time trying it. After a while, I noticed nothing was happening. I got annoyed so I searched the house for the guy and told him the drug wasn't working. He started yelling and cursing at me because I accused him of giving me fake stuff. He brought other kids over to show me how tweaked out they were and said they all took the same thing. Neither of us could explain why it wasn't working for me though. He gave me another one. I took it. And thirty minutes later, nothing. Seriously? It was crazy!

He gave me another one. I took it. And thirty minutes later, still nothing.

Then, suddenly, I felt a heavy sense of conviction and guilt come over me. The hairs stood up on the back of my neck. I never experienced anything like that before and didn't tell anyone, because, well to be honest, I was dumbfounded myself. A few minutes later, the burden turned to what I can only describe as a voice telling me to "Go home." I smoked a lot of weed that night and was extremely high. But damn, not that high to hear voices. Sure, I was appalled that the LSD wasn't working, but now this. Then . . . it hit me. I knew exactly what was going on, and boy I was upset.

I looked up and said, "Really?" As soon as I said that I felt it again, "GO HOME!" I thought, *Wow! Ok.*

I knew in that moment God was telling me, "Enough is enough. Take your butt home; this is not your scene."

He had to be the reason the LSD wasn't working; there was no other explanation. Then to get such a profound feeling that I was to go home, it all began making more and more sense. By the time I got home, it was past one a.m. For a 12-year-old kid, that was late, especially when my parents didn't know where I was. Before I walked to my room, I peaked in my parents' room and sure enough . . .

There she was—my mom was on her knees, praying.

Ok, you must first understand something. My entire life, when my mom is on her knees praying, the impossible always seemed to happen. I watched it dozens of times myself, miracle after miracle. My mom is the fiercest prayer warrior I've ever seen. That night, her focus was on me; and it worked! I couldn't explain what I was feeling as I stared at my mom on that floor. Perhaps I should have been thankful for God saving me from a tragedy that could have happened that night, but instead I was angry that He ruined my high.

Out of spite, after that experience, I lost it. I spiraled so fast and was successfully fashioning a dangerous lifestyle for myself. Not by mistake either, as I did things no child should do. Ever! Partying with people twice my age, being exposed to dangerous situations I had no business being a part of. By the time I realized things needed to change, I didn't know how to make the spiraling stop. At times, there were glimpses of what I thought was a light at the end of a dark tunnel, but it seemed like the closer I got to the light, the farther away it appeared.

What was I going to do? I felt hopeless. If I was going to get myself out of the situation, I needed resources, but I didn't have any. Eventually, the stinging of the lifestyle I chose started to feel normal again. I accepted the fact that nothing was going to change, so I learned to keep quiet and taught myself to hide. I became exceptionally good at hiding and extremely hard to read. People tried, but the wall I built around myself was so thick that no one could get through it. I made sure of it.

WHY THIS STORY?

This story was a pivotal moment in my life. As you read on, you will learn more about my childhood. Like many of you, I lived through a lot of hate, pain, and confusion. I lived with an unshaken feeling of no self-worth that shaped the decisions I made growing up: those decisions killed me emotionally, mentally, and almost physically.

The truth is, no matter what you have gone through, you're still alive. Take comfort in that. Yes, you have been passed over, ridiculed, and counted out. And if you're reading this book, chances are you're frustrated that you haven't become the person you know you can be. Rest assured, a shift is coming. Change is inevitable; are you prepared to receive it?

THE MOVE THAT CHANGED EVERYTHING

Up until that moment our living condition was ok. Sure, I was doing things I shouldn't have but I never had to worry about where I would sleep. Then we moved and I learned that it would be the last time I'd live in a house for a long time. We experienced difficulties that many of you would consider unimaginable. I was mortified to tell my friends where I lived, humiliated to tell anyone where I lived. In fact, this is the first time I'm sharing this part of my story, and it's been thirty years.

So . . . here it goes. My dad has always been a dreamer, and his dream was to build us a house. He was stoked when he found a piece of land in Rio Rancho, New Mexico, located just outside of Albuquerque.

It was a one-acre lot he bought as soon as he could afford it. In the dead of winter every weekend, depending on how much money he made at work, and after paying the bills and buying food, he used whatever he had left to build the first room of the amazing house he visualized. It took him months.

Eventually, the money he "had left" ran out. We lost the rental home we lived in as well, so my parents were forced to move the entire family into the room my dad framed on that lot. Yes, I said framed! It was a wood-framed room. Truthfully, it was more like a shed, measuring no more than 300 square feet. To eat, my mom cooked outside using a small single burner propane stove. There was no electricity or running water. No sink, no bathroom, just a room full of furniture and bags of clothes.

Have you ever sat and wondered how much water you consume daily? Probably not. Why would you? I never did, until water became scarce. When you don't have easy access to basic needs like water, you tend to think about it more. Everyday water is used for brushing teeth, drinking, cooking, bathing, and washing clothes, dishes, hands, and for cleaning. For us, getting water was difficult. I don't remember the details of where my parents went to get our water. I assume they probably filled up five-gallon jugs at Walmart.

Who knows, but we stored clean water in a Home Depot bucket, and then covered it up until we needed to use it. Getting ready for school was rough. It started with waking up in sub-zero degree weather. To brush my teeth, I filled up a small cup with freezing cold water and used the same cold water to wash my face. Bathing was the worst of all; we reserved a corner of the room to shower. Well, I can hardly call it a shower, to be honest. It was more like cleaning-the-important-parts-of-your-body-type of shower.

I used a cup to pour cold water over myself as I washed with a bar of soap. Come to think of it, I wonder if that's the reason why today I love scalding hot water. The sobering part of bathing like this was my mom had to hold a towel over her head to cover my naked body while my siblings sat just feet away, looking the other way to give me privacy.

Living like we did, in the winter, when it's snowing outside, it was brutal to say the least.

By now you're wondering where we went to use the restroom. I don't think I need to share details about that. Use your imagination, but I will say it was a humbling experience.

After what felt like years of living outside, I was happy to move out of the shed. My father opened a church in downtown Albuquerque, so we moved into that building instead. The shed and the church were equally challenging to live in, but at least in the church we had heat and air conditioning.

Once everyone was settled in, I had to get creative on how to live in the new building. The bathroom was small in the church. It was a typical bathroom you'd see in a retail building, with a toilet and a small sink.

That's it! No shower, but at least there was a door for privacy.

The best part I'd say was having warm water. Although I still used a cup to pour water on my body to shower, considering what I experienced in the shed, showering at church was an improvement. Undoubtedly, the worst part was not having a bed. In the shed, we put mattresses on the floor. But living in a church building, we couldn't bring the mattresses because there was nowhere to store them. Plus, my parents didn't want people to find out we were living there. My parents left it up to us to be creative. We each picked what was comfortable for us to sleep on. Everyone was different.

For me, first, I pulled together six black metal chairs. For it to work, all the chairs had to face each other to create a flat surface. I used a comforter, sheets and pillows to cover the seats on the chairs. Falling asleep wasn't bad; the challenge was staying asleep. If I moved, the chairs began to pull apart from each other. And, well . . . Crash! Every night, there I went, falling to the floor in my sleep. It was horrible. I slept like this for hundreds of nights. Besides living in a church building, don't forget it's still a church, a place where people gathered every week to hold church services.

CHURCH

If you go to church on Sundays, you know the routine. You and your family take a typical weekly trip to the church building, followed by attending a one hour-and-fifteen-minute service. After church, you sometimes go to a restaurant, you enjoy a nice lunch with your family, and then you head home. Am I right?

Well, my weekly routine was far from ordinary. Sundays, my dad hosted two services, one in the morning and one in the evening. The entire family had to get up at the crack of dawn, get ready, and eat breakfast. Everything had to be done early so we had enough time to clean up after ourselves and hide all the evidence that we lived in the building. When we were done, we helped my parents line up the chairs and clean them. Then we sanitized the entire building to prepare for service.

Did I mention that in Brazil, there's no such thing as an hour-and-fifteen-minute church service? Service ended when the time felt right. Most often, they lasted over two hours. As everyone was going home after the first service, we'd leave with them. This was the only time we'd go out to eat. Typically, we'd stop at McDonalds or another place that was inexpensive. After lunch, we'd head back home to the church building. We had a few hours to unwind, and then repeat the process over again for the evening service.

I'm not sure what happened, and I didn't care to ask but my dad either lost the building or he needed a larger space. But next we moved to another church building not far from the first one in downtown Albuquerque. The living accommodations were pretty much the same, except the new location was much larger and there were separate office spaces we shared as bedrooms. Oh, and this one had a kitchen, so that was good, really good. No more cooking on a single propane burner and living out of stacked up Tupperware containers for kitchen cabinets.

THE HEART OF THE POOR

Every Sunday, after church, my parents hosted a drive for the homeless. During the week, people from the congregation talked to friends and family to figure out what was needed; then they went to local yard sales and collected clothes for women, men, and children. They also collected shoes, jackets, and toys. For food, everyone brought different types of cooking ingredients to the church. After service, they cooked up massive amounts of food.

As the homeless came to the church, they helped themselves to anything they needed, and they ate as much as they wanted. My dad's church helped hundreds of homeless people on a monthly basis. My mom, of course, was in her happy place, without a doubt. Even today, she loves talking to strangers and ministering to them. On days we didn't see many homeless come through the church, my mom walked to the local park and told everyone to come eat and get new clothes. If there was leftover food, my mom and her friends hit the streets, holding plates of food to feed everyone else that didn't make it to the drive.

I can only imagine the courage my parents had to have to organize something like that every week. Helping the community the way they did, knowing the living conditions they themselves were living in with their own family, that speaks volumes about their characters. What's even more fascinating is I never heard my parents complain about our living situation. Whenever us kids said anything bad, they reminded us that we had food to eat and a roof over our heads. They were always so thankful for what they had. The sad part is my dad never got to build the dream house he always talked about. He never made enough money to do it.

THE SHOP

Despite the failed dream of building a house, my dad had another dream. The dream was to start a business. He invested everything he had to open his first company, which was an auto body repair shop.

He named it 7-Stars to represent his seven children. The trials my dad faced were unimaginable. Naturally, every business owner reading this would understand.

The hurdles often felt like they were impossible to jump over, and he encountered every difficult incident you can humanly conceive.

But my dad never gave up.

He experimented a lot, looking for middle ground. His world was blurry, but he kept a clear head and was always searching for clarity. He devised every plan imaginable to pull us from the rubble.

But soon after opening the shop, my dad's church closed. I don't remember all the details, but I suppose he couldn't afford the rent for the church building because he spent it all starting the business. I could be wrong but in either case, once again we didn't have a place to live so we all moved into the body shop and lived there for a while.

The overwhelming struggles that came from following a vision and searching for his purpose in life became heavy for my dad. I watched him day after day fill up his calendar with business meetings. He was driving from place to place, attempting to learn the ins and outs of operating a business in the United States. It's almost as if he was constantly in panic mode, and maybe he felt like if the panic stopped, then the dream would stop and die with it. So he kept going.

Knowing what I know today and understanding what it takes to operate a business, I wonder if even though I was out living my life as a pesky teenager, I must have subconsciously been paying attention to what worked and what didn't work in my dad's company and churches. Is it safe to say that opening a church and starting a business is one and the same?

Sure, one is a non-profit organization while the other is a for-profit business. The structures are different, but the expectations are the same. What I mean by that is, in either case, there are systems one must implement for any operation to succeed. There's also a level of promoting knowledge one can't go without if they want to inspire others to support them. Just a thought. My father didn't have these systems in place which is why he struggled so much.

My dad trained all three of my brothers to work in the trade. He taught them everything he knew about the car industry. And although 7-Stars eventually went out of business, the knowledge he shared remained. Today, my three brothers and my dad operate a successful body shop in South Florida. The shop has been in business for over twenty years.

My mom, despite all the chaos of starting life over in a strange town, supported my dad in all his ideas, even if it meant suffering for them.

7
CHOICES

DARKEST MOMENTS

My living situation, my experiences, my trials, my rebellions, and my struggles, although difficult as all hell, have made my existence in life so much clearer. My father never had the resources to do what he was called to do for the people of Albuquerque. I'm the last born of the family, and I believe God has given me these resources. I can't imagine that it all happened by accident.

The way I see it is we are all born for a reason, for a vision, for a purpose. And it's our job to find out who we are as people. It's our job to chase that vision and fulfill that purpose. I believe everyone is capable, capable of making a change. And, more often than not, the crazy people are the ones who believe they can change their cities. Change the world. Well . . . I'm crazy! Crazy because I have no doubt in my mind that I can change Albuquerque. Change the world.

However, before a person is capable of provoking change, I believe they first must live through a level of difficulty best described as their "darkest moments." It's the time in a person's life where they felt so alone the silence was deafening. The sheer obligation of living through that type of silence is what later guides them in fulfilling the purpose they were born to fulfill.

I understand this sounds harsh and cruel, and perhaps hostile, but bear with me and let me explain.

I told you earlier that in this book I would share with you what I believe my purpose is, and I believe I have many. One of them is to help young women during their darkest moments in life and help them to see a way out, so they aren't forced to make decisions that could potentially alter their family lineage.

Many of these young women may have already experienced circumstances worse than I did but like I said before, and learned the hard way,

---

I won't reduce my life experiences based on someone else's.

Just because someone had it worse than me doesn't mean I had it good either. It's not a competition; everyone handles struggle different, and that's okay. We are to walk our own paths in life, and it's those paths that shape who we are.

WHY IS THIS SO HARD

This chapter by far is already the hardest for me because my darkest moment starts here. I'm vacationing in Hawaii right now and had every intention to finish writing this book during the trip. Well, that didn't happen. Not because I procrastinated or delayed working on it, because I worked on it a lot. And got a lot done, but I knew that to finish the book, I'd have to get through the next two chapters where I share my darkest moments growing up. Instead of bulldozing through it, most of the trip I went back to read and edit the previous chapters before continuing. But then I reached a point where I couldn't edit the chapters anymore. Now I have to get to the meat of my story.

Before I started writing it all down, I closed my laptop and took one final break. I had to do something to prepare my mind for this. So, my husband and I took the kids to a place called Ho'opi'i Falls in Kauai. It truly was a remarkable experience. There are two waterfalls there, and both require some hiking to get to them. The hike itself is beautiful, but the waterfalls added an exclamation point to what was already an incredible day out. At the first waterfall, we all had an opportunity to jump off a cliff. The kids went first. And one by one, they jumped without hesitation. Next went my husband, and he too jumped without a second thought.

I, on the other hand, could not jump. As soon as I looked down and saw the distance of the water, I froze and was truly petrified. My legs were shaking so bad, I ended up causing a scene. There were at least eight people at the bottom, sitting on the rocks and looking up at me, and another four behind me waiting for me to jump so they could go next. The situation became a spectacle, with everyone screaming and cheering me on, telling me to jump. One man was signaling me to take deep breaths before jumping and assured me everything was going to be okay.

It was silly. Even though I watched a dozen people do it before me, I was still scared. My legs shook so bad that later that evening, my daughter Brielle told me that it looked like the Holy Spirit grabbed a hold of me. Ha ha! I laughed so hard at that joke. The show went on for almost seven minutes. Seven minutes!

The reason I know that is because my youngest daughter Deja recorded the entire thing. Finally, I took a deep breath, made the decision to jump, plugged my nose, and took the plunge. Ahh!

And I did it.

I faced my fear and overcame it. Later that day, I played back the video and as I took the leap, everyone was cheering. My kids were yelling, "Go, Mom." It was cool. I tell you that story because it's what encouraged me to push through the noise in my head and write about the next phase of my story. Believe it or not, documenting the experience I had on that cliff inspired me to finish this book, just so I can say I did it. I faced my fear and overcame it.

THE STRUGGLE

So much of the chaos that happened in my life happened before I turned eighteen. It was a struggle, and I say struggle because I was not only trying to find myself but I was also learning to forgive myself at the same time. However, I can't say the latter occurred quickly; it took decades. I lived through decades of not forgiving myself for the decisions I made growing up.

Do you remember when you turned thirteen? It's assumed to be a fun year because you finally became a teenager. That part of a pre-teen's life is supposed to be exciting and elating, the year you begin to learn who you are. You realize what motivates you and what stimulates your senses. When I turned thirteen, things began to settle down. After three years of living in commercial buildings and a shed, my parents found a house.

I was excited for this new chapter but unfortunately, things didn't settle down; the opposite happened.

Thirteen was the year I wish I could take back. I was in eighth grade and was still doing all the crazy things I talked about in earlier chapters, but that year the type of friends I made changed drastically. Inching closer to high school, the decisions I made began to show itself in a big way.

Not in a good way either. I was a hot-tempered teenager. I wasn't violent, as I never liked violence. I just talked a lot of trash. Maybe that was my way of protecting myself, my way of coping with my atmosphere. The school I went to was teeming with a multitude of gangs. It was typical to be asked, "Where you from?" Your response was indicative of which gang you belonged to. Kids everywhere confidently asked strangers everywhere they went. I was fascinated by how proudly they asserted their allegiance.

Being surrounded by gangs is one thing; becoming a part of one is another story. There were a few kids pressuring me to join but I always told them no. I had no intention of becoming that person. I assumed I was a prime target because I talked a lot of crap to people and was good at it. But I knew that I was not cut out to be a gangster. One afternoon, I was walking in between the outdoor barracks building to get to class when suddenly, I was struck on the back of my head. I immediately fell to the ground. As I hit the floor, people began punching me and kicking me everywhere. There was not an inch of my body that wasn't trampled on. All I could do at that moment was cover my face and take the beating.

When the pounding stopped, I got up and saw two girls and a guy standing in front of me. The look they had in their eyes was terrifying. It's almost as if they became something else for a moment. Then it happened. They asked me the dreaded question, "Where you from?" I wanted so badly to say nowhere.

They jumped me. I never asked to be ranked into their gang. But nonetheless, I had to decide. I knew that if I said nowhere, it would only be days before I got shot and killed for disrespecting their family. So, in fear, I replied and said what they wanted to hear, asserting the allegiance they wanted me to say.

The next several months, I witnessed so much disregard for human life. I was scared to get close to people because as soon as I grew to love someone, they were killed by a rival gang. Kids were getting paralyzed. Kids were getting kidnapped, never to be seen again. Kids were found dead in ditches. Terrified doesn't begin to describe my state of mind. I frantically needed someone to talk to. I couldn't go to my parents, as I felt I was too far gone. If I told my siblings, they would tell my parents so that was a dead end. I was too young to ask friends for advice. And the adults I surrounded myself with weren't any better. You remember the story about the father of the girl I met in the sixth grade and him getting me high?

I didn't want to do that again!

That year, my sister Soraya got a job at a community center down the street from our house. In my effort to escape the violence, I began hanging out at the community center and befriended the adults that worked there. Every day after school, I sat in the office and talked to the employees and drank coffee. All of them were old enough to be my parents. I opened up to them about what was going on in my life. But I only shared bits and pieces here and there, never too many details because I didn't want anyone to know what I was really thinking. Being high every minute of the day didn't help either, but smoking helped me cope. It kept my right mind from attacking my conscience.

FRIEND OR FOE

My sister and I befriended one of the guys that played basketball at the community center. I can't remember if he was an employee or just went there to play. But he always had a friend with him, a super shy quiet guy. It started as an innocent friendship with the guys. They were older than us, I remember that for sure. At the time I didn't know how much older, but I didn't care to ask. The four of us sparked a close friendship. The basketball player gave us rides to the community center after school, fed us when we were hungry, and took us out for ice cream.

He did a lot for us, but nothing inappropriate ever took place when we were with them. Even our conversations were innocent. For the first time in a long time, I felt safe. Then out of nowhere, one day, my sister told me that something wasn't right;

---

she was getting a bad feeling when we were with them.

Of course, I thought she was crazy. She insisted and pleaded that I stop hanging out with them. But I didn't listen.

Eventually, she pulled away completely, and it was just me hanging out with them. After a while, I invited another friend of mine to take my sister's place. We were having so much fun together with the guys: going to the movies, even taking short trips out of town together. Of course, my parents had no idea what was going on, especially not where I was going. When I'd call my mom to tell her I was okay, I'd assured her I would be home soon. I never cared to give her details of what I was doing or who I was with. Looking back now, I cannot imagine what must have been going through her mind. How could I have been so insensitive? I was completely oblivious to her feelings, totally unaffected by her concern for me.

My mom was genuine, honest, and caring. And I trampled her with my disrespect. Man, I was such an ass. The tears are building up in my eyes just writing this. Eventually, one by one—my friend—then his friend—stopped hanging out with us. But I wasn't affected by it. He was a good friend so the two of us started hanging out alone. The innocent conversations soon turned to kissing, then making out. But he never touched me inappropriately. Eventually, the innocent kissing turned into me sneaking out of the house at night to see him. What was I thinking?

8

MY FAITH SAVED MY LIFE

FOE

One evening, this friend of mine picked me up for what he called a special evening. I believe we went out to dinner and a movie but I honestly can't remember because it turned out to be a tragic night. Looking back now, I see why I blocked out so many details of that night because, frankly, it was a disaster.

By the time the guy friend and I were done with whatever we did that night, it was late. He suggested I spend the night at his house because he didn't want to get me in trouble if he dropped me off at home that late, or that early, I should say. He told me his mom was home and suggested he'd sleep on the couch and I could sleep in his room. The plan sounded okay to me. It was the first time I went to his house, but we'd done sleepovers before when we traveled out of town with the four of us and nothing ever happened. We always slept in different rooms. I convinced myself he had never overstepped his boundary before, so why would he start now?

He pulled up to the front of the house and slowly parked the car. I opened the door, stepped out, and closed the door behind me. He waited for me as I exited the car, then we walked to the front of the house together. As we walked in the front door, he softly spoke out, "Hey Ma. I'm home. Don't get up; I'm going to bed. Good night." He showed me to his room, showed me where everything was, kissed me on the forehead, and said goodnight. I felt awkward sleeping there. But eventually, the self-conscious feeling faded, and I fell fast asleep.

Suddenly I felt someone crawling in the bed with me. Dazed and confused, I slowly attempted to wake myself up to awareness. Before I realized who was crawling in the bed, he began to kiss me. But this time, the kiss felt different than before. Something was off; something was wrong. He was more forceful than he'd been before. I got scared, really scared. I said, "Stop! What are you doing? Get off!" He started to powerfully grope my breast. He was pushing on it so hard, it hurt. With every push, his breath became heavier and heavier.

The way his body pressed on mine made it hard for me to breathe.

"You're hurting me," I told him. "Please stop!" But he wouldn't. Then he whispered in my ear, "Take off your pants." I panicked. I know he heard the fear in my voice when I told him, "NO." Then, the look on his face changed. His eyes became dark, malevolent. His lips started to move, as I heard the words, "If you don't take your pants off, I will. And you won't like the way I do it." That's when it hit me; this man is going to take every ounce of dignity I have left. Terrified, I slowly began to slide my pants over my hips, then down the sides of my thighs. Then my legs. The only piece of clothing left was my under-wear. Such a minor piece of fabric suddenly symbolized my self-worth. As it slowly rolled down my body like a scroll my value rolled away with it.

As his body entered my virgin body, I was tormented by the pain.

My insides felt like they were being ripped apart.

Back and forth, his strokes grew faster and faster. I never cried so hard in my life. When he was finished, he got up, put his clothes back on, and, without uttering a word, walked out of the room.

I cried and cried and cried.

When the sun rose, he came into the room and said it was time to go. I felt so defeated. Overpowered, crushed and overcome with horror as I walked to the car. The ride home was dark and somber. I turned my body away from his. If I pushed any harder on the car door, I was convinced I would fall out. Maybe I should have just fallen out. It would've saved me from what came next.

He turned on a song for me to listen to, which was *Down Low* by R. Kelly. Some of you may remember that song well. I can hear the lyrics playing in my head like it was yesterday. The song talks about keeping a bad action on the down low. It describes the action as creepin'. Then it talks about how nobody has to know. How fitting right? Of course, he didn't want anybody to know. The next day, I didn't know what else to do so I did my best to act normal. I pretended like nothing happened. I quickly learned how to hide, from myself, from my feelings, from my turmoil. I felt so ashamed. I went to school and continued to pretend like things were okay. After school, I went back to the community center. Perhaps I was putting up a front, ignoring the fact that I was raped. I felt that if anyone found out they would blame me, so like the song said, I kept it on the down low.

MY FOE BECAME MY ENEMY. MY ENEMY WAS ME.

At the community center, the next day, that same man, my foe, came up to me and told me to get in the car. I asked him where we were going, but he didn't reply. As I followed him to the car, I wondered, *Is this what an abusive relationship feels like?* Despite what he did to me, I went anyway because I was afraid of him. I was petrified by the thought that he would tell people what happened and somehow turn it on me.

I convinced myself what happened was my fault.

After all, I put myself there; I didn't listen to my sister's warning. Surely, I deserved it, right? It took me many years to accept that it wasn't my fault. I was thirteen!

In the car, we didn't go far. He pulled and parked in the parking lot of an old, beat-up, and dirty motel. He then walked around to the passenger door, opened it, grabbed my hand, and took me up the stairs to the motel's second floor. He walked me down a long outdoor hallway and into a small room that smelled musty, like old, damp sheets. It was the type of place you expected to see in a movie, a place where prostitutes worked. He pulled me onto the bed and started to grope me just like he did before.

What was I thinking? Why was I there? How can I allow myself to be in this situation…? Again! It was almost as if I became the foe. I became my own worst enemy. When he finished, we immediately left the room and got back into the car. And just like before, the ride back, this time to the community center, was dark, somber, and quiet.

My body turned away from his again as I pushed up against the car door. I looked out the window and wondered what my future would look like. *What person was I becoming?* Those were not thoughts a thirteen-year-old should be having. Never saying a word, he turned on the same song for me to listen to from R. Kelly. When we got back to the community center, we walked inside. He never spoke to me again after that.

Looking back now, I am so thankful he never again uttered a word toward me. For starters, I was thirteen. People have told me they believed he was twenty-six at the time when this happened. I'm not sure, but does it even matter?

I recently heard a story of a teenage prostitute from Oakland. Like me, she was vulnerable, running away from the hardships she was facing in her life and looking for love in all the wrong places. Like me, she was thirteen when she was raped. Except immediately after, her abuser took her to Figueroa Street in Los Angeles, 372 miles away. There, he beat her until she submitted to prostitute herself. Every dime she made selling her body and doing unspeakable acts to hundreds of men on the streets, she gave to her abuser. Her foe. Her rapist. Her pimp. She became pregnant at fourteen and gave birth to a son at fifteen. She was sixteen when she shared her story with a youtuber that interviews prostitutes and pimps in LA. She shared how she had hopes of working as a makeup artist and nail tech, with the dream to own a nail salon.

I can't help but think just how easy it would have been for my foe to do the same to me. I honestly can't sit here and tell you that I would have fought tooth and nail to run away from that man. Just imagine for a minute if he swooped me up and taken me to Los Angeles like the young girl I just talked about? I certainly would not be here today telling you my story.

This man, he methodically hooked me in. He oh so vigilantly waited for me to let my guard down.

The wall I worked so hard to build up around me was being taken down one brick at a time. As soon as I was at my breaking point and most vulnerable, he pounced.

It was a brilliant plan of deception. Disgusting, but brilliant.

The shame was unbearable. I reached my lowest point and was desperate, even suicidal. For over a week, no one knew what happened to me. So, I asked my parents if I could stay at my older sister's house for a few days. She lived in an adobe home. If you've never seen an adobe home, the walls are made from clay, sand, and silt, which makes for a perfect, soundproof room. I locked myself in the room. For days, my sister had no idea I was crying, moaning, weeping, and sobbing as I repeatedly punched the walls.

As the blood rolled down the white walls, the pain I felt on my knuckles, just for a second, made me forget the pain I was feeling everywhere else. When my sister realized what was happening, she found a way to open the door. She was in shock when she saw the bloody walls and knew immediately that something was wrong. Clearly. I blanked out after that. I cannot remember a word I said to her after she asked me what happened. Of course, she told my parents, who wanted to press charges. But I begged them not to. For the rest of my middle school year and high school years, I didn't want to be known as the girl that got raped. Who knows how long I would have survived that?

My parents agreed not to press charges. But within weeks, my parents sent me to live with my other sister in South Florida. I lived there for almost a year.

LIVING IN MY DARKEST MOMENT

Finally, I was back in my home state of Florida, the only place I felt safe. I smelled the salt in the air. The ocean breeze hugged me ever so gently again. However, the feeling of being home didn't last long though. I noticed something was off; things were different. I realized that this time, there was no safety. There was no security. The air smelled the same and the breeze felt the same.

Except, I wasn't the same. I was a new person, a broken person. I was disoriented. Lost. Someone with no self-worth. I was living in my darkest moment.

I endured a sense of loneliness, and the silence was deafening.

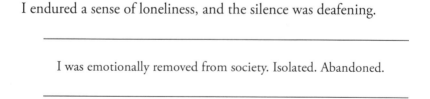

I was emotionally removed from society. Isolated. Abandoned.

I didn't have anything else to live for. The only thing I could turn to at that point, frankly, was my faith. I had nothing else. I remembered what my mom told me when I was younger, "God always provides. Remember that when you get older."

Hmm, God always provides. Those words played over and over in my mind—provide. What does that even mean? It means to supply or make available; to make preparation to meet a need.[1] Well, I was in desperate need of supply. I wasn't prepared to meet my need, and I mentally wasn't available for anything. In fact, I wasn't capable of doing anything good or productive. The silence in my head was so loud, I would've done anything to make it stop. Anything!

Even if it meant my heart stopped with it, if my heart stopped, my mind would stop. My thoughts would stop. But that couldn't be the way I was going to live. Thinking like that! What was wrong with me?

That's when I pressed into my faith like never before. I started listening to sermons and sing songs that encouraged me. I also prayed. A lot! Believe me when I say if I didn't have my faith to lean on, I would not be alive today to write about it.

9
THE SCALES IN MY EYES

JUST A GLIMPSE

In Florida, one of my sisters owned a duplex and the people that lived next door were her friends. Their ten-year-old daughter came over after school, and I'd babysit her until her parents came home from work.

After the year I just had I needed some me time. One Friday, I was doing a lot of praying. In fact, I was fasting. If you don't know what that is, it's when you sacrifice something you need or want so that you can focus on what's important at that moment in your life. Then you expectantly pray and make your petition, your request, to God.

At that time in my life, I was looking for clarity. My future felt bleak, and I needed answers. Fast! While I was praying and asking God to show me what my future looked like, I began to see myself helping young women navigate through difficult life situations. I wanted to warn them somehow, warn them of the foe's that pretend to be friends. I wanted to show them how they could prevent the downward spiral in their lives. And for those that were already living in their darkest moments I wanted to teach them how to get out.

I knew I couldn't be the only girl going through what I was going through, and I wanted to save them from the agony I was experiencing. That afternoon, when the little girl came over, I was sitting in front of the TV watching a live church service. The little girl was standing behind me near the kitchen counter. As I sat, intently listening, I suddenly felt a shift in the atmosphere. The hairs on the back of my neck stood up. Something wasn't right. I turned around, and I looked at the little girl. The look on her face was different too.

Her eyes were dark and malevolent. Wait! I've seen this before!

It was at that moment I realized what was happening. Just like my dad experienced in the most pivotal moment of his life, this had to be mine.

The little girl stared at me. Then, with a snarky look on her face, she said, "You know, something is telling me to grab a knife and kill you right now." I was dumbfounded. The darkness I saw in the man that took my dignity; I was seeing in this little girl too. But wait, I thought I got away from that evil. What was happening?

Why was I being tormented?

Despite my hindrance, I understood what was happening. The story my dad shared with me popped in my head as the little girl stood there with a disgusting look on her face. I knew it wasn't her talking! She had no idea what was going on. She didn't know what I was going through, or what I was doing that day. The little girl had no clue that through my prayers, I was receiving clarity to help other young women like me. The torment had to be something else.

I believe when you have a powerful purpose to fulfill, you will immediately be faced with adversity.

Adversity is the enemy of truth, and that enemy doesn't want you to succeed. That enemy doesn't want you to believe that you can change. That enemy doesn't want you to know that you have the power to help others, to change someone's life for the better.

Well, I'm here to tell you that enemy is a liar.

As I sat there, staring at the little girl, thoughts came rushing into my mind like a flood. Then I drew up the nerve to respond. I struck back and said, "Oh yea? Well, I know who you are, and you know you don't have the authority to be here." When I said those words with confidence, knowing and understanding that the enemy doesn't have authority over me or my purpose, she snapped out of it. Then she started to cry and asked me, "What happened?"

Now what? I didn't know what to say. What do you tell a child when they've been used by a demonic spirit to attack another human being? I didn't want to scare her, so I said, "Nothing, you're fine." That Friday afternoon, sitting there with that little girl, was the day I believe I found my purpose; I was fourteen. It was odd to me, realizing that immediately after I found clarity on my purpose, suddenly something so nefarious occurred. Even though I felt angry, disorderly, adrift, and abandoned, somehow, just somehow, I knew my purpose was to help young women just like me. I was burdened by the thought that someway I had to figure out how to teach them to escape the chaos. Escape the silence. The self-inflicted abuse. Escape the prison that they all held themselves in.

But how? I didn't have anything to offer them. I was just a kid! I called my parents and told them what happened with the little girl. The next day, my dad was in the car, driving from Albuquerque to Florida to pick me up.

NO JUDGEMENT

I know what you're thinking. Wow, this chick is crazy, and she wants to project that crazy onto others? That's not the case at all! In fact, I don't consider myself crazy at all. I have discernment. I have a relationship with Jesus. There's a difference. I had to lean on my faith, if not that what else then? I had nothing else going for me. But don't you think it's odd that so far in my stories, it seems like the more I leaned on my faith the harder things got? The more clarity I got on my calling the nefarious thing happened. I don't believe in coincidences, not like this anyway.

Don't judge me for leaning on my faith when life got so hard, I didn't know what else to do. Don't judge me for leaning on my faith when I felt hopeless and had nothing good to look forward to. Don't judge me for leaning on my faith when it felt like taking my life was the only option I had. I wouldn't judge you for the decisions you made in your life that helped you cope. I bet some of those things seemed crazy to you too.

Let me ask you a question, what do you think I mean by when I say help girls like me? When I say my purpose is to help young women? Well, I'm not talking about religion or even spirituality, in fact the help I'm talking about is a concrete set of resources that is tangible: help they can see, feel, and touch. It's the type of help no one can take away from them. I didn't have this resource to offer when I was younger but now, I do, so why not use it to change a generation. To give back in ways I never thought possible.

I may have discernment in many situations in my life. And yes, I'm in tuned with my spirituality, but who isn't? Even if you call yourself an atheist, you are in tuned with something. Aren't you? Be honest with yourself. There must be a level of solace, peace, and understanding you rely on, right? I'm sure of it! Each one of us have given this type of peace a name. Mine is Jesus. What's yours?

Wherever you are in your walk of life, I know that deep down you wonder what your purpose is too.

Why are you here? I've said it before, and I'll say it again.

The only thing that makes you different than me is your experiences.

74

And how you interpret your experiences is what makes you who you are. In this book, I'm sharing with you my experiences. And those experiences are what made me who I am.

Yes, my faith is important to me. It's the only thing that has gotten me through the difficult stretches of my life. But it's not just faith that helps people. It's resources. Opportunities. Second chances. Confidence.

Self-worth.

Back then, I didn't have any of that. How could I help young women? At what capacity would I be able to help anyone? After what just happened to me, did I even want the headache? After all, I just lived through a little girl telling me she wanted to kill me. Seriously? You would think that would have motivated me. But the opposite happened. On the ride home, back to Albuquerque, I talked to my dad about what happened. I was vague though; I shared the details of what the little girl said to me, but I didn't say anything about the newfound purpose I discovered.

I was embarrassed to share that part. I was a nobody, just a kid looking for answers. I wanted nothing to do with it. So, I did what any four-teen-year-old would do. I ran. I ran from the idea that I even had a purpose. It was too much. That was nearly thirty years ago, and I've been running ever since.

That was until I began writing this book. Reliving my story, being open with you about who I am brings me back to that little girl that had nothing to offer the world. This book allowed me to confront that little girl. She was sitting on a curb holding her face in her hands not knowing how she was going to pull through. I quietly approached and sat beside her. Inching closer and closer, I leaned in and said,

"Lift up your head. You are here for a reason. You are not a nobody; you are being prepared and preserved for young women that are not even born yet. The clarity you just received is being saved for a time when the world will need it most. When that time comes you will share yourself with the world and it will be epic."

BABY LOVE

When my dad and I arrived back in Albuquerque, I tried to find some level of normalcy again. So, I tried out for the cheerleading team in my high school. I was so proud when I learned I made the cut. My sister Soraya was a junior in high school. She told me about a guy in her class that had a crush on me. She asked me to go to homecoming with him. My immediate response was, "Heck no!". First off, I was not attracted to him at all. He was 6'4" and wore high water pants. She pleaded and begged me to do it. In the end, I caved and went to homecoming with the guy anyway. He turned out to be okay, I guess. He was funny and had a good personality. After homecoming, we started hanging out more.

Because of my last experience with a man, when things started to get serious, I didn't know how to handle it, so I got mean. I pushed him away, I ran from him in the hallways, hiding during passing periods. Poor guy. He was trying so hard. Then one night, he told me enough was enough. He turned on a song while we sat in the car and stepped out so I could listen to it by myself. The song was about a man that loved a girl, but she wasn't serious about his feelings, so he had no other choice but to let her go.

Dang! Not bad for a seventeen-year-old kid. After that day, I was all in. We became inseparable. He was the first man I allowed to touch me in two years. In fact, I think we were nominated, in the yearbook, for the couple that would make it. Ha! Didn't happen because I was walking to class one day after lunch and saw him coming out of a corner rubbing his lips after kissing on some chick. I was shattered.

In fact, I never even told him it was over; I just never spoke to him again. He tried to get my attention here and there, but one thing I don't tolerate is cheating. The disrespect speaks louder than words. Soon after that, with the same girl he kissed, they were nine months away from becoming parents. Boy did I dodge a bullet! Phew!

It was for but a moment. I felt happy, as I loved that man. You know what I'm talking about, right? That high school fling many of us had.

The love is intense, so intense you never forget it. But when you get older, you're thankful it didn't work out. The sad part for me was, I was 0 for 2. Both men that I let my guard down with betrayed me.

MY FRIENDS WEREN'T MY FRIENDS AT ALL

For a long time after that experience, I hated men. All men. I hated what they were doing to me. I hated how they made me feel about myself. I hated that I wasn't good enough for them. So, hurting them became my new happy. I was determined. So much so, they became my target. First, I made them like me. Then as they fell harder and harder, I dropped them like a bad habit. One guy cried. He was so upset that I hurt his feelings, he asked what was wrong with me. He told me I was mean and didn't understand how I could be so cold.

The way I saw it, in my sixteen-year-old mind, he didn't deserve to know why I was being so cold. Who was he anyway? He was just a man. And men do it to women all the time. Why is it that when women do it to them, we're labeled as cold-hearted? So, I told him to stop crying, and stop being a little B @#$%. By the time I was seventeen, my idea of coping was to become someone else. To surround myself with people that were hurting just like me. Part of that was becoming a heavy alcohol drinker and a chain cigarette smoker. I progressed past marijuana and began trying other drugs, like cocaine and mushrooms.

Through all that, there were two situations that got me thinking. During those two situations, I began to realize that my friends weren't my friends at all. And my little vendetta for men wasn't going to get me anywhere. I was pissing off a lot of people.

The first situation was a girl at school that thought I was after her boyfriend. I don't know if she heard about my reputation with guys, but it got to the point where she was determined to fight me. The talk of this fight spread like wildfire; it attracted dozens of kids outside after school one day. But before the fight began, I caught a glimpse of a reflective piece of glass she was holding in her hand. Apparently, she intended on cutting up my face. When I saw the glass, I called her a coward for not fighting with her hands and walked away. She still got the fight she wanted that day; it just wasn't with me.

The second situation was a bad encounter with hallucinogenic mushrooms. I was at a friend's house when someone came over with a new kind of mushrooms we hadn't tried before. Of course, we all put our hands out to try it. To be safe, I suggested that we stay at the house when our trip started. Everyone seemed to agree; that was until we all ate it of course. The thought of tripping out during a movie would be cool. I was the only person with a car, and I fell for the idea that I could drive to the theater before any of us began to hallucinate. That was a terrible decision.

We all quickly jumped in my car, and I drove as fast as I could. Halfway there, while on the freeway, suddenly the curb began to move like a snake. The taillights and headlights of the cars on the freeway started zipping back and forth at light speed. I started to panic. Instead of going to the movies, my friend told me drive to her cousin's house so we could get off the highway.

When we pulled up to her cousin's house, we noticed all the lights were off. Then her cousin came outside, whispering. I didn't know what was going on. When we got inside the house, her cousin told us that there was a drive-by the night before, so they had to keep all the lights off to make the perpetrators think no one was home. Are you kidding me!?! I wanted to get out of there as fast as feasibly possible. Then her cousin asked me to drop him off at the hotel down the street, so I jumped to my feet.

That was my ticket to leave. We both got in the car, then suddenly everyone else jumped in with us. When we arrived at the hotel, her cousin asked me to wait for him while he ran inside to get something.

Suddenly, a car pulled up next to us. Two men were inside wearing bandanas. They gave me a dirty look and drove off. That's when her cousin ran out of the hotel, jumped in my car, and told me to drive. The two men suddenly turned around and began chasing us and shooting at us. I thought I was going to die that night. I don't know how long the chase lasted but somehow, I managed to lose them and immediately took everyone to my friend's house and told them to get out of my car.

Can you believe they got mad at me for "ending the party early"? Are you kidding? What party? We almost got killed. What would have happened if those men caught up to us? They surely weren't our friends.

I know what you're thinking. I probably hallucinated the entire story. I don't know, maybe you're right, but that experience was enough for me to cut all ties to every single person I called a "friend" at the time. The scales in my eyes were beginning to fall off. The rest of my time in high school, I isolated myself. I talked to no one and decided to concentrate on my schoolwork, except that decision was made too late. I was so behind on credits, and there was nothing I could do to make it up before graduation. So, I was forced to settle for a GED.

10

CHANGE IS FINALLY HERE

A FRIEND'S SAVING GRACE

Since I knew I wasn't going to graduate, I made an unambiguous decision to help a friend escape a dangerous situation. She had a bright future in sports but got caught up with the wrong guy. She got pregnant and ran away from home to live with her boyfriend. Once she was fully engulfed in his environment, he became extremely abusive. She showed up to school with bruises on her face, arms, and legs, never the belly though. After months of witnessing this, I was done.

I made it my duty to get her out of that house of terror. I picked her up for school each morning at sunrise. Before going on job interviews, I advocated for her, telling the interviewer that they had to hire us together. I would not accept a job unless she was hired with me. There were at least three employers that accepted my condition. For months, after school, I took her to get something to eat. Then we'd go straight to work. After work, I found other things for us to do so I didn't have to take her home. By the time I dropped her off at his house, it was so late he was sleeping.

Her boyfriend knew what I was doing and hated me for it. But I didn't care; I wasn't intimidated by him. I knew that he wouldn't dare touch me. Of course, my loudmouth helped. I wasn't timid like she was around him. He wasn't my abuser; he was hers. Finally, one day I convinced her to leave. She, her mom, and I planned her escape for over a week. Every day when I picked her up for school, she packed clothes. That way when the day came, she didn't have so much to pack all at once.

On a Friday afternoon, while her boyfriend was away and the house was empty, we packed up all her belongings and she went back home. She was eight months pregnant. Looking back now, as I tell this story, it never occurred to me that I was living my purpose by helping my friend escape an impossible situation.

Shortly after that, we got jobs at MCI together. For those that don't know what that is, MCI was a telemarketing company that sold long-distance minutes to customers with landlines. Landlines are phones that you plug into a phone jack in your house. In case you didn't know. Lol! Working at MCI turned out to be the best decision I made. My life was about to take a dramatic turn in the right direction. Before I get to the MCI story though, allow me to paint this picture for you.

CRUSH

In high school, there was a hallway that all the jock guys hung out at. It was one of the main hallways, so they had front-row seats to watch all the girls walking to class. It was nerve-wrecking walking down that hallway, but many girls liked the attention. For me, there was one boy in particular that I noticed. He was the quiet one, a senior.

I never heard him say a word when all the jocks were hollering at the girls walking by. He was very polite. I loved that about him. And let me tell you, he was drop-dead gorgeous.

He had the most beautiful green eyes.

Anyone that knew me knew I had a massive crush on him. But my sister's friends, however, were older, and made fun of me for liking the hottest guy in school. One girl told me that I was not his type, and he would never go for a girl like me.

Really!?! Why are girls so mean to each other? I was so hurt by her comment.

The last day of school, I was holding a stack of wallet-sized prom photos of my boyfriend and I when the green-eyed boy walked up to me and asked if he could have one. My entire body went numb. I couldn't feel my knees, and my voice cracked when I uttered the words, "Yea, sure." After he graduated, I saw him around a few times. I tried getting his attention, but he did exactly what my sister's friend said.

He never gave me the time of day. In fact, one time he called his girl-friend as I was sitting next to him trying to strike a conversation. Damn! It's like that? But that just made me like him even more because he was faithful and respectful. Eventually, I gave up and moved on. I guess I wasn't his type after all.

So, the first day of training at MCI, as my friend and I walked into the training room, what do you know? Lo and behold, the green-eyed boy was sitting in the room. My friend tugged on my arm and said, "OMG! Danny is here." My heart sank. I couldn't believe it; I was starstruck. He still looked good as ever of course, except this time I kept my distance. I didn't try to get his attention. We worked on different teams, but we saw each other during lunch breaks. We started having light conversations here and there.

Then one day, I was walking past his cubicle, and he slipped me a note.

My knees buckled. I was so nervous, I took the note and kept walking. I was trying not to make it look like I was tense. *Why would he slip me a note? What did it say? Oh, my goodness!* The walk back to my cubicle suddenly seemed like it was miles away. I immediately sat down when I got to my desk. I took a deep breath and opened the note. The note read: *"If you're not dating anyone, can I take you out to dinner? Please circle Yes or No"* My heart leaped.

O . . .M . . .G . . . I couldn't believe it. He asked me out. I was smiling so big my jaw hurt. I didn't circle yes or no. Instead, my response was, *"It's about F @#$%&* time."*

We went on our first date a few days later. It was incredible! We talked for hours. From that day on, we were inseparable. We did everything together. This was it; I could feel it.

HE WAS THE ONE

My crush became the love of my life. It's been twenty-two years since our first date, and I still get butterflies when he walks into a room. Remember that dinner I told you about where my sister shared how we got to the States? That same night, she told me another story I never heard before, and it had to do with my husband, Danny.

My family was having dinner at my sister Eklesia's house, and I wanted them to meet Danny, so I invited him to come over. When we walked into the house, it was the first time my mom laid eyes on him and apparently, she knew he would be my husband. She signaled my sister Eklesia to come to the kitchen. Then she whispered,

---

"That's him, that's him! That's the man I've been praying for. He's Priscilla's husband."

I always wondered why after dinner that night, my sister told me not to mess this one up. Lol! It was my mom that told her to say that.

We were madly in love. And as you might imagine, two young love-birds who were madly in love, what do you think they're doing on

84

their free time? You guessed it; we were having sex. Of course, my parents didn't know but they soon found out because two months after we started dating, I got pregnant.

I'll never forget the day we went to the store to buy the pregnancy test. We were sitting in the car as I read the directions on the pregnancy test box. Danny had his phone on his lap, when suddenly we heard a voice that appeared to be far away, saying, "Hello, hello?" It was his dad on the phone. Eek! Apparently, Danny dialed his dad's phone number by mistake. We were so scared that his dad heard our conversation. But Danny was convinced his dad didn't hear anything, so we went inside, and I took the test.

As we waited for the result, I told him, "If it's positive, do not ask me to marry you just because I'm pregnant." I wanted him to stay with me because he wanted to, not because he felt like he had to. Fifteen minutes later, we both slowly leaned in to see the results. And there it was, two bright red lines showed up on the test stick, clearly indicating that we were expecting. I was rattled! I keenly looked at the test again, then looked at Danny, then at the test again. I was so overwhelmed I didn't know what to say.

Just then, I noticed that Danny was doing the same thing I was, except he keenly looked up at me after seeing the results and said, "Will you marry me?"

Holy moly! Now I was really flustered. I looked down at the test again and back at him again, and the first thing I could think to say was, "No!"

Then I said, "Wait, that's not what I meant. Yes! Wait! Did you only ask because I'm pregnant?"

Poor guy, he didn't know how to respond to my reaction. I think I hurt his feelings when I said no the first time. It was an incredible night full of surprises. In the weeks ahead, some family members didn't take the news very well. I know they were just as scared as we were. In fact, some even suggested I get an abortion.

"You're too young," they said. "You don't have any money. You don't even have a career. There's no way you can provide for a kid."

To be honest, the thought of abortion never crossed my mind. Yes, I was only eighteen, and I didn't have anything to offer a child. But I felt like if I thought I was grown enough to be having sex, then I was grown enough to be a mom. After all, isn't that what happens when you have sex?

Instead of fearing about what I couldn't provide, I shifted my focus to what do I need to do to provide?

There was no other option. Some frowned upon my decision but what those people didn't understand was this pregnancy, this massive, fearful moment in my life, in all honesty is what saved my life.

MY BOYS

A few weeks after finding out we were expecting, we searched for a place to live. One of the places we looked at, the leasing agent told me I would be good at the job she was doing. I never thought about working in multi-family apartment leasing. I told her I would think about it. Then, she said that employees got a 20% discount on the rent. *Um! What!?! Sold! I'm in! Where do I sign?*

Weeks later, we moved in, I applied for the job, and I was hired. The only thing left to do was to prepare to meet our son, Nakqi. We were so young and had no idea what we were doing. But the one thing we both agreed on was we both needed to work hard to provide for this beautiful, little boy. On August 26, 2000, Danny and I got married in his parents' backyard. I was eighteen, six months pregnant, and, for the first time in my life, I was looking forward to my future.

So, there I was, new job, new mom, and married to an amazing man. Wow! God is so good!

My life took a sharp turn from just the year before when I was in utter desperation. I was living in fear of not knowing what my life would be like and scared of the direction I was going in.

But God!

My mom's prayers yet again came to the rescue. She prayed for the man I would one day get to call my husband and declared it when she first laid eyes on Danny. My heart was full. My husband and little boy took me by surprise. And boy, was I thankful they did.

MY NEW FAMILY

In the next several years, our family grew. First came Nakqi; the little boy with the biggest smile and a heart that that changed everything for me. Two and half years later came Brielle; the sweetest independent baby girl that loved to sleep and make grown up decisions. And four years after that came Deja; the easiest to give birth to, the kindest and most loving baby girl that since the day she was born already loved helping people. Our family was complete. I worked in multi-family property management for thirteen years, as Danny and I decided that I would not be a stay-at-home mom. I wanted to provide for my kids in a different way.

For years I was basically working for experience and never for a paycheck because my entire paycheck went to paying for a good daycare, one that offered a curriculum that prepared the kids for kindergarten. Today, I can say it was the best decision I made. By the time I was twenty-five, I had three kids. My focus was placed on how I could be a role model to them. I wanted them to grow up seeing their mom work hard and go after the things she wanted. I wanted them to see that I was able to obtain the things I set my mind to and teach them that they can do the same for themselves when they're older.

I wanted to teach them that even when life throws you difficult stretches, you should never give up, or made to feel like you have to make decisions other people want you to make.

I was determined to show them that the hardest decisions they would have to make are often the best ones, and to not be afraid to make them.

No matter what happens, God will be there, walking beside them and preparing them for the best part of their lives, as well as the worst.

I want my children to embrace the hard times. I learned that my hard times prepared me for my purpose in life. My prayer for my children is that they will fulfill their purposes. I pray that they don't have to wait till they're in their forties to find it.

Go after what you want! Work hard. Be respectful. Put God first. And don't ever apologize for being who you are.

11

MY FIRST CAREER

PROPERTY MANAGEMENT

When I started my career in property management, my starting salary was $7 an hour, so you can imagine how far the 20% discount on our rent went. In terms of experience and life lessons, I would say that the decision to start a career in the multi-family industry turned out to be a good one. However, the way I exited that career was one of the hardest circumstances I ever endured. In fact, because of the level of stress I was in at that time in my career, I lost out on my entire thirtieth birth year. What do I mean by that?

Two things:

One: Twenty-nine was the last year I remember enjoying a career I was good at. Sometimes, even when you're good at something, your asset can quickly become your liability.

Two: Except for my career ending, I literally don't remember anything else that happened the entire year I was thirty. It sounds crazy, but it's true. Hear me out.

I was wishing my sister Soraya a happy birthday and asked her how it felt to be thirty-one. She looked at me and started laughing. Then she said, "Priscilla, I'm thirty-two and you're thirty-one." Huh? "Ok, sure," I said, then I started laughing too. We went back and forth for a few minutes. She had to show me the math for me to believe what she was saying. And she was right! I did turn thirty-one that year, but I don't remember ever turning thirty. How does something like that even happen? How does someone forget an entire year? I suppose it was a coping mechanism to the trauma I experienced.

Perhaps it was my brain's way of enduring a treacherous period in my life. Don't worry; I won't leave you hanging. I will explain what happened in that period in chapter 14.

Just so you understand, property management was the first time in my life, besides being a mom and a wife, that I put my all into anything. There were ups and downs of course like any other job, except for me, I felt like no matter what happened, I didn't have an option to leave. Ever! It was one of those industries that if you overcame the challenges and got good at it, it paid extremely well. And for someone like me, no experience or degree, opportunities like that doesn't come around often.

I made a choice, and I had to stick with it. And I did! There was no other alternative. I wanted to quit dozens of times, but for my new family's sake, I had to make it work. I had to. The field came with possibilities for growth, so I didn't want to miss out on the opportunity to manage my own property one day. So, I stuck it out for thirteen years.

WHERE IT STARTED

The first property I worked at was the largest property in Albuquerque at the time. It had a total of 572 units, two large clubhouses, a gym, two pools, and more. The size of team it took to maintain the operations for a property that size was massive. In the office, starting from the top, there was a:

- Property manager
- Assistant manager
- Marketing manager
- Leasing manager and
- Five leasing consultants
- Not to mention the eight-plus person maintenance team

For the business to succeed, the management team also had to succeed, and the leasing team was no exception. Our leasing manager was tough. She had extremely high expectations for us.

Her name was Liz and, in her eyes, there was no room for failure. Laziness was never an option and downtime, ha, downtime didn't exist.

The challenge for me was little Nakqi, growing inside me, loved to eat. I was always hungry; never in my life did I experience hunger pains the way I did when I was pregnant.

Every hour, on the hour, without fail, my stomach burned with hunger. It felt as if I hadn't eaten for days. So, every hour, I snuck away for a few minutes to snack on whatever I can put my hands on. I made sure to always be mindful and respect the busyness of the office. When I saw someone walking in, I'd immediately put my food down and greet them.

Liz had a thing for meeting clients at the door. She believed that was the only way to display optimal customer service. If clients weren't immediately greeted, she lost it. Literally, she lost it. The leasing office opened at 8 a.m. Back then, there was no internet so if you wanted to get information on an apartment, you had to drive to it to see it. Every day, there were at least ten people standing outside waiting for us to open. So, you can imagine how hard it was to sneak away to eat.

Liz couldn't stand my snack breaks; it made her furious. I didn't want to hide from her but every time I wanted to eat, it felt like she was sensing my hunger pains too. Whenever I disappeared, even for a minute, she intently walked around the massive leasing office looking for me. Then sure enough, when she found me, she yelled, "Get back to work! We don't have time for you to take breaks like this. There's a lot of work to do."

She hated my breaks so much that she started adding up all the mini breaks I took and told me if I reached an hour, she was going to count it as my lunch. I felt so condemned. Seriously though, it wasn't my fault I was hungry. There was no way I could control it. How else was I supposed to feed my son? My number one priority was to take care of my baby.

To be completely honest, I could not stand Liz. She was too much. No matter how hard I worked, she was never happy.

One day I was in the assistant manager's office, eating a yogurt. There were no prospects or residents in the office at the time. The office had a large glass window as one of the walls, facing the hallway leading into the leasing office. If someone walked in, there was no way I'd miss them. Liz was on the other side of the building walking around. When she saw the reflection on the glass of me standing there eating, she immediately changed directions and headed toward me. "Priscilla! You're eating again?" she yelled. "I've had it with you. That's it, I will get you fired for this."

After months of abuse, walking on eggshells, and in fear for my job every day, I scheduled a meeting with the property manager to ask for a transfer. I remember there being a sound of desperation and fear in my voice when I spoke to her. I waited for weeks, then finally, a position opened. I hated Liz for putting me through such misery during my pregnancy. I was pleased when the day came that I was cleared to move properties.

Seven years had passed, and the property I managed had a team of twelve people. My leasing staff were all away showing apartments one day when I heard the door chime go off. Right away, I stood up and started walking down a long hallway that led toward the front door. Before I even got to the hallway, I heard footsteps. As I turned the corner, there she was, Liz, in all her glory. Believe it or not, after years of being in the industry, when I had my own property, I learned to respect Liz. I appreciated her love for greatness. It was her high standards that helped me succeed in that business as fast as I did.

She was wearing a black skirt and a green sheer blouse tucked tightly around her waist. Her hair hadn't changed a bit: straight, dark black, and shoulder length. Her hair was swaying back and forth as she walked toward me.

"Priscilla? I didn't expect to see you here. Congratulations, you're a manager. Except you took too long to get to the door. Did you not learn anything I taught you? Prospects shouldn't have to wait to be greeted."

I was flabbergasted. As soon as I saw her, my heart sank, and I immediately went back to feeling like the eighteen-year-old getting in trouble all over again. It made me nervous. But for what? I was a grown woman, so why did I feel anxious? I had to respond to her. But how? What do I say to the women that terrified me when I was eighteen, but was thankful for years later? When my mouth finally opened, I said, "Liz? Hi, yes ma'am, you're right. I'll be better next time."

That's it? Wow, that's all I could muster up to say to her. Whatever, I'll take it.

That day was my chance to say what was on my mind, to tell her how she made me feel when I was younger but also thank her for being tough on me. Anxiety is real, even though I had all the right words in my head, my instinct simply wanted the anxiety to go away, so I froze. Frankly, even though I grew to respect Liz, at the time, I believed she wouldn't have received the compliment if I told her. Liz was very private and didn't dare show her feelings to anyone. It was black and white, hot or cold, and nothing in between, which is what made her so intimidating.

What I didn't know was, that would be the last time I'd ever see Liz. The next time I heard her name, a few, short years later, was from someone telling me that she got sick and passed away. I was sad when I heard the news. That women trained so many young ladies in the property management industry. I can only imagine, but my guess is that many of them were top leasers that all became amazing managers. I admire her discipline and drive toward a career she loved so much. She taught me to work hard and never to make excuses. She believed that providing the highest level of customer service is what ultimately brings high levels of success to anyone. Today, I know that is one-hundred percent true.

Thank you, Liz, for being so hard on me at the beginning of my career. I was too afraid to tell you, but I believe you saw something in me that I didn't recognize in myself. Much of the fearless businesswomen I am today is because of you. I won't forget the impact you've had in my life.

Rest in peace.

THE SET-UP

For thirteen years, I worked my way up the corporate ladder. Like I mentioned before, despite the difficulties, the industry offered such a high level of opportunity and growth that I couldn't just walk away. By the time I was twenty-three years old, I was managing multi-million-dollar properties, the daily operations, and their financial assets.

Finally, I found something I was good at. Something I can be proud of myself for. I found fulfillment in ways I hadn't experienced before. I was honored, admired, and reverenced by the work that I was doing. I became very good at my job. The industry just made sense to me. I loved everything about it! All the details, the systems, and the projects: I submerged myself in it!

For years, I didn't have to apply at jobs. I showed up to interviews and was hired on the spot. I had a reputation of getting things done. Yes, I was a young mom, but because Danny was so supportive, I was able to grow my career beyond what I could ever imagine. But as you know, often with success comes:

- Jealousy
- Hatred
- Manipulation and
- Deceit

The backstabbing in that industry was on another level. The minute you became competition to someone, the claws came out. Except the interesting thing was many knew that you knew what they were doing, yet they didn't care. They'd smile to your face after doing unthinkable things that costed your job.

I was just a baby when I started, walking out of a life-threatening and underprivileged lifestyle.

Property management presented new levels of struggles for me, struggles I never experienced before. However, as grim as it may have been at the time, it forced me to believe in and trust myself. I became the only person I could rely on. It taught me to be vigilant and wary. I became attentive in my decisions, and today, I am exceptionally observant and alert.

And I owe that to the lessons I learned working with women in power.

After all, being watchful and cautious never hurt anyone, right?

12

WOMEN IN POWER

THE MANIPULATOR

One of the properties I managed at the time was known to not be a good one. It was old, mismanaged, and falling apart. I was the type of manager that took pride in my properties, no matter how old they were or what kind of reputation it had. I treated it like my own. Always! When I arrived there, the property was losing millions of dollars. My team and I worked diligently on the property, and for the first time in a long time, the property was making money. My leasing team was rocking it too. The property was maintaining an occupancy rate of over 95%.

The owners loved it, but as you can imagine, I was being put on a pedestal and some people around me, not everyone, began to treat me as if I was showboating. I wasn't showboating; I simply loved my job. No matter how large my team was, I worked well with them. I was tough, I had high expectations. Hmm! Come to think of it, I became my own version of Liz. The difference though was I worked with my team. Wherever there was a shortage, I filled in; Liz didn't do that. I painted apartments, unclogged toilets, patched holes on walls, cleaned pools, scrubbed tiles, cleaned gutters, painted curbs. The list goes on.

I suppose that perhaps managers and supervisors that were around me weren't doing those things so it's easy to imagine now, in hindsight, why they hated me. Maybe I was making them look bad. Who knows, I'm guessing. The property had just undergone a property inspection with the owners. They were extremely pleased with the direction the property was headed in.

It was the end of the year, after the inspection, when I had a meeting with my supervisor to discuss which invoices I was going to pay for the current year and which ones I was going to hold off to submit for the following budget year.

Submission of invoices were extremely important in that industry. Certain projects were budgeted for certain months, so you had to be careful to pay them according to the month the budgeted income was available. My supervisor and I went through each and every single invoice that was scheduled to be paid. After our meeting, I had a stack of invoices to process that day, December 31st. Then the following day, January 1st, we agreed I was to submit the other stack.

On January 2nd, out of nowhere, my supervisor showed up at my property and fired me.

Are you kidding me? Why is this happening? I'd never been in trouble before, let alone terminated. Why was this happening?

What did I do?

I demanded a reason for the termination. The property was doing incredibly well; my team was amazing. We were all having so much fun working together and succeeding together. As I was packing my things, my supervisor sat in my office watching me. However, something wasn't right. I noticed that she was having a hard time looking in my eyes. So, I pressed into that! I looked at her and asked her why she was terminating me; it was manipulation at its finest. You would never guess what she told me. "I fired you because you held invoices from last year and didn't pay them."

What!!! You . . . have . . . got . . . to . . . be . . . kidding . . . ME!

At that moment, I knew what was happening. There was no point in arguing. It wasn't going to change the fact that I was losing my job; it was her word against mine. I looked her in the eyes, standing there, in silence, as I processed what was happening. She knew that I knew exactly what she was doing. I finished packing my things, hugged my team, and left.

THE DECEIVER

The next company was much smaller compared to other companies I worked for prior. I thought that by doing that, the so-called competition and backstabbing I experienced before was less likely to happen. Unfortunately, I was wrong. Like in years past, the property I was hired to manage was not making any money. In fact, the occupancy rate was sitting somewhere in the 70% range. In that industry, that number is awful. Normally, owners prefer that the occupancy rate rest at or above 94%.

Like before, I put everything I had into the property; I respected the challenge. It was something to look forward to, an incredibly large project that when finished would be exceptionally rewarding.

In less than a year, my team increased the occupancy rate to 98%.

When it came time to do the property inspection, I was bummed to be out of town. A few months after the inspection, the owner wanted me transferred to another property he owned so that I could do the same thing for him there. It was a much larger property, larger team, and more work in terms of re-organization. The existing system operations they were using to operate the property were in complete disarray.

Nonetheless, it was the challenging type of environment I flourished in. And I was excited to start.

This time it was different. Fixing that property was going slower than I anticipated. The re-organization of the systems was an astoundingly time-consuming thing to change. Then suddenly, I started to see a shift in the way my supervisor interacted with me. Whenever she'd come to the property, she would have a team meeting and scold everyone in the room, telling us that all we had was that job; we didn't have a backup plan for survival. Then she'd follow up that statement by telling us she had a backup plan for her life and we weren't going to mess that up for her.

The strain my team was under was unacceptable, and it was rubbing off on me, and not because of anything I did. They were terrified of my supervisor, so much so that it became impossible for me to manage them, which was further impacting our progress. Our results. The pressure turned to stress, the stress to anxiety, then eventually to a heaviness I couldn't control. That was the first time, since my teenage years, I started to smoke again. I hated the person I was becoming. Something had to change.

Well, it didn't take long until I had a meeting with my supervisor about invoices that needed to be processed and submitted during a certain period on the property budget.

Again, with invoices? Looking back now, it seems as if claiming that a manager was holding bills was the go-to for supervisors that wanted a manager out.

The day I had the meeting with my supervisor, she cleared an amount for me to process for a large remodeling project we were doing at the property. I explained to her that the amount she was clearing was going to leave a lot of bills still owed to the vendors.

She told me that it was fine, and that the rest could be submitted "later." I wrote down the number so I wouldn't forget and immediately shared the information with my assistant manager, the person that was processing the invoices for me. When "later" arrived, the following month, I called my supervisor to get approval on submitting the remainder of what was owed. Her response was appalling. She began yelling at me and accusing me of holding the information from her.

Really?

Before telling my assistant manager what was happening, I asked her to write me a statement of what her understanding was of the situation regarding the invoices for the project. She wrote the statement, and when I read it, it was exactly the way I remembered.

After what happened last time, I was not going to be deceived again. This time, I fought back!

The next day, I called my supervisor and told her what I did and told her I had a written statement from my assistant manager regarding the matter. According to her, she didn't care about the statement. She told me that she was going to talk to her boss and the owner of the property and told me to be prepared because there was a good chance I would be terminated. The fascinating thing, though, was that suddenly she was speaking very softly. She wasn't upset and rude like the day before.

This time during our conversation, she made a complete shift, she sounded concerned and acted upset at the chance that I could get terminated. She even got emotional, assuring me that it was an honest mistake. She gave me the impression that she was going to fight on my behalf. Wow, I couldn't believe it! Am I going crazy or was this woman going to be supportive? Maybe she remembered our conversation after all? A few days passed, and she called me. She said she spoke to the team and asked me to come to her office for a meeting. I was nervous. How was this going to go? Even though I believed she'd advocate for me, I was anxious to see how the conversation with her supervisor and the owner went.

When I arrived, I was ready. Because of what happened before, I was ready to be let go. When I sat down at her desk, the look she had on her face was terrifying. She seemed to be so angry. I thought to myself, *Welp, this is it; here we go again, I'm done. The owners didn't care what she had to say.*

No matter how much I applied myself to my career and maintained a high level of honesty with people, it was never enough.

I immediately became angry and annoyed that the owners wouldn't accept her advocation for me. I was thinking, *How could they be so cruel?*

Then she started talking. Believe it or not, the conversation took a sharp turn. Word for word here is what came out of her mouth. I was astonished!

She said, "I spoke to my boss, and I spoke to the owner of the property as well. What you did was wrong. You made me look bad, and I am pissed off. I want so badly to fire you right now. My boss agrees with me and believes you should be fired too. But fortunate for you, the owner hates me and loves you and what you have done for his property. God must be on your side chick because the owner will not let me fire you."

I didn't know what to say. I couldn't help but wonder three things:

1. Was she annoyed because I covered my ass and had a true written statement of what really happened the day we spoke about the invoices?
2. Was she mad at herself for the fact that she dropped the ball? And couldn't place the blame on someone else? Or;
3. Was she livid that she was looking for a reason to get rid of me and her scheme didn't work?

Perhaps it was all three? Who knows, but believe me when I tell you, after this meeting she made my life a living hell. If she couldn't fire me, she was going to, somehow, make me quit. Love of the owner or not, she had the power. And in the end, she won. I quit!

I didn't quit because I gave in to her, like you're thinking. I quit because I was becoming someone I didn't like. The stress was making me hate life, the way I was mistreating people because of my environment was wrong. I was under so much stress; I was taking it out of everyone around me.

When I left, I made a vow to never again treat my team like dirt again. Unfortunately, before I left the property management industry, making the decision to be nice brought about another level of betrayal, one that I wouldn't wish on my worst enemy. This leads to my third and final story, and the reason I left property management for good.

I guess being too soft makes you a doormat, and doormats get stepped on.

13
THE INSPIRER

ROLE MODEL

For this final property management story to make sense, I have to take you back for a moment. Back to the beginning. After working with Liz (you remember Liz?), I found a great company to work for. Everything about this company I loved, so much so that overall, during my tenure in the industry, I worked for them for seven of the thirteen years. I was twenty years old when I met the company's regional manager, who oversaw the properties in New Mexico. At the time, if my memory serves me well, it was seven properties total.

The minute I laid eyes on her; I knew I wanted to be just like her. Her name was Rae. She carried herself so gracefully, speaking softly and always eloquently.

Rae displayed a level professionalism and confidence I admired.

It was then that my focus shifted. I set a target to become a regional manager one day and I was willing to work hard to get it. I knew the steps I needed to take to achieve my goal. The positions I needed to excel in.

Leasing Agent—Leasing Manager—Assistant Manager—Property Manager—Regional Manager

One day, Rae gave me the single best piece of advice anyone ever gave me. She told me that to be noticed for a promotion, I needed to not only excel in the current position I held, but also, simultaneously, excel in the position that I was seeking to be in. Even though it may not my role, I may not be getting paid to do the work either, but she said I needed to show that I was able to handle both roles before I would be looked at for a promotion.

And so, I began my journey in becoming a regional manager. For the duration of my time working under Rae, I was fortunate enough to experience the progression of my career the way I did. It was a development I could be proud of:

- First and foremost, of course, I started working as a leasing agent, leasing apartments at a 250-or-so unit property. There I was able to better grasp the position of a leasing professional because, unlike working with Liz, I was the only leaser. And because of that, I was dually learning the assistant manager responsibilities as well.
- When I grasped both roles well, I applied for an assistant manager position at another property. It was a much larger property, over 400 units.

REALITY STARTS TO SET IN

I was so happy when Rae told me I got the job! Naturally, the promotion came with challenges; one of the main challenges was learning about myself and figuring out how I fit in. Everything about the new property was high-end, and I didn't know how to conduct myself in that type of environment. Up to this point, the properties I worked at were in bad parts of town. The exposure was far from high end. In this new atmosphere, I didn't know how to dress professionally, plus I'd get nervous when residents came in using big words that I didn't understand. In fact, my new manager held team meetings talking about what people on the team were "wearing," saying it was ghetto and inappropriate. Yes! She said ghetto. In one of the meetings, she called out people wearing cargo pants. I immediately knew she was referring to me, as no one else on the office team wore cargo pants but me.

I was so humiliated.

Another time I was using the front leasing desk computer. Not knowing that my manager was using it just before I sat down, I opened our software system, only to find an email she was sending to another manager.

In it, they were talking about me, laughing at the way I looked and how I spoke.

I remember the words on the screen like it was yesterday; the conversation went like this:

She's nice and all but way too rough around the edges. Yea! she's so ghetto. I know, it's sad, she doesn't even know how to speak to people. I think she's uneducated. Oh, and what about her clothes? Oh, my goodness, the clothes. It's so embarrassing.

I was so hurt when I saw these messages on the screen. If I had any confidence from being promoted, it was all gone now. That evening, I went home and told my husband Danny I needed a new wardrobe. The following weekend, I opened a JC Penney credit card and stocked up my closet with professional attire, pant/skirt suits, and high heels. Next, I intently started to observe the actions of every person that walked through the door: residents, vendors, employees, property owners, regional managers, you name it.

I studied their mannerisms and carefully observed the language they used when they spoke. Then I'd look up those words to find its meaning.

I was determined to get it right and had an unwavering desire to simply be seen and respected.

But, besides studying people how do I do that? I remembered the advice Rae gave me on how to get promotions, so I sought to obtain my own property. I convinced myself that was the only way I wouldn't have to deal with the disrespect because I'd be in charge.

As an assistant manager wanting to be a manager, I had to make myself stand out. Right, so what did I do?

1. I mapped out my day to be as efficient as possible. First, I reserved the morning hours before lunch to lease apartments. Then after lunch, I concentrated on my assistant manager duties. As an assistant, I was responsible for all the money transactions, making deposits, data entry, and maintaining, and organizing resident files, leases and property reports.
2. I made sure to win all the leasing contests my manager put out. It infuriated the leasing team but hey, step up your game.
3. Then, I went to my manager and told her I wanted more responsibilities. Gradually, she saw that I was reliable, consistent, and hungry to learn, so she allowed me to do most of her responsibilities. All she did was sign off on things to submit to Rae. The only thing I didn't do was be in meetings with upper management. Everything else, I handled.
4. I went to work as early as I could, after taking the kids to school. The days that Danny could pick up the kids from school and feed them dinner, I made sure to work late so that I could get all my work done. Sometimes that meant I worked till 10pm.

Finally, all my hard work paid off! I not only mastered two positions like Rae recommended; I mastered three. I was the top leaser, I knew my assistant manager duties like the back of my hand, and I made my manager's job exceptionally easy by taking as much responsibility as I could off her shoulders. After months of doing this, Rae called me into her office and offered me a promotion to a larger property, working as an assistant manager. It was a lateral move technically, but there was a catch. The manager of the property just left for a three-month maternity leave, when, suddenly, her assistant manager walked out.

So not only was I being promoted to be the assistant at a larger property, but I was also being asked to simultaneously be the acting manager as well. It was a 500-unit property; larger team, no one knew me.

That's a tough thing to do. Rae must have known that I was nervous, so she gave me the second-best piece of advice I'd ever gotten. She said, *"never turn down a promotion or a good opportunity, no matter how hard it is or how scared you may be."* With that, I accepted the promotion.

Taking on the role of assistant manager and manager that year, I was nominated assistant manager of the year for the role I played in overseeing the 500-unit property. After all that hard work, a position to become a manager came up within the company, and I applied for it. Unfortunately, Rae overlooked me for the position. I was devastated! Why was I still not good enough? She told me another assistant manager was next in line because she'd been with the company longer.

I was so hurt by the ordeal that I applied for a manager position with other companies and was offered my own property somewhere else. Finally, my own property. I was a manager!

I quit working for Rae and went down my own path working for other companies. I was twenty-three years old at the time.

It was hard: the companies weren't the same; the people weren't the same. For the first time, I saw the corruption that took place in the industry. My property maintained a 94% occupancy. However, the company wanted my property operating at 96%.

Other managers were all maintaining their occupancy rates at 96-98%. I couldn't understand how they were doing it. I seriously, for the life of me, could not figure out how it was possible when the market averages that year was 94-95%. Months on end I was being hard on myself, thinking that perhaps maybe I wasn't good at this at all. When I finally had the chance to spend some time at another property, I learned that the manager was fudging the numbers. Can you believe it? I couldn't! I never would have thought that was normal.

Lying at that scale when you're managing someone else's multi-million-dollar asset?

Nope, I couldn't! I wouldn't! It wasn't worth the risk. No wonder their numbers were always so pristine. It was all a lie. How fair was it that I was maintaining what most would consider an excellent occupancy rate, without fudging numbers, yet I was getting scolded daily by my lack of performance?

When I realized what was happening, I knew I was in trouble. The manager that was fudging the numbers was so confident that she shared what she was doing with me. She insisted that it was fine. In fact, this was the way she thought of it, saying, "What they're asking for is impossible! And I'm not going to risk my job to do the right thing when they can care less about me or my family. So, I'm going to give them what they want."

Despite her reasoning, I didn't agree. I told her that I couldn't operate like that and was going to keep my numbers true to what it was. She didn't show it at the time but those were my final last words. Now she had an enemy, someone who knew the truth of what she was doing. After our conversation, during our manager conference calls, she'd question the performance of my property, humiliating me in front of the entire team of managers and owners. Eventually, her tactics succeeded in me losing my credibility with the regional manager. The day came when both showed up to my property without notice, called me into the conference room, and proceeded to write me up for not meeting expectations.

Wow! Just wow! Not meeting expectations. The woman that cheats and lies on her reports to make herself look good to the owners is

Ok, I got it!

My assistant manager, Jewel, was a single mom to the cutest, little girl. Jewel and I had an amazing friendship. I admired her work ethic and her passion for the career. I trusted her.

She'd always put her best foot forward and helped me tremendously with the team. After a while, I hired my niece's boyfriend Liam to work for me because he also had an amazing work ethic. Of course, I had to speak to Rae about it before I hired him, since I knew him prior. Nothing new; that's what you do in the corporate world.

My niece and Liam weren't engaged or married so he wasn't related to me, per se. But in either case, I felt more comfortable knowing that she knew I knew him. In fact, over the course of the time I was there, eventually everyone knew who he was to me because the relationship he had with my niece started getting serious. Rae even attended the church Liam and my niece went to, and watched Liam sing on the worship team. I was proud of the team I put together.

For the next two years, things were going so well. The property was undergoing a massive remodel, and I was learning the ins and outs of project management on a different scale. I loved it.

Until one day, it all came to a screeching halt.

THE TIDAL WAVE HIT

I was in my office early one morning when I heard Jewel's panicked voice say, "What? There's no way. There's no way. It's zero?" I wasn't sure what she was talking about until she came to my office. She said she was taking money out of the laundry machine, but it was empty. It was Monday morning, so not having money in the machine was impossible. Residents used the machine all weekend to do laundry. The total displayed on the machine, she said (if my mind serves me well) was $1200 collected in cash. This never happened before.

Someone stole from the company.

I thought, truly, that can't be right. Our team was too tight knit for something like that to take place. Or at least I thought.

That same week, I was scheduled to go out of town for a managers retreat. I told Jewel that I didn't want to create a scene until we knew for sure what was happening. I thought that if we locked the process down, kept our eyes peeled, and observed everything that had to do with the possibility of a theft, perhaps we will find out what was going on. Thieves do stupid things, so in my mind I thought surely, they'll do it again and we'd find out who took it.

I was gone three days, to which Jewel and I communicated non-stop.

But there was nothing else out of the ordinary happening while I was gone. The daily deposits were all matching. Maybe it was a one-time thing, which, in either case, I'd have to report it. When I returned from the retreat, Jewel did another withdrawal, counted it, and it all matched up nicely again. It was a Friday morning, and I told her to put the deposit in the safe. Then I told her, before she went home for the day, to take the deposit to the bank, since the next day was Saturday, and the bank was closed. On Monday morning, I heard Jewel, again, saying, "Oh no, no way! No way!" So, I asked her, "What now?"

She said she forgot to take the deposit to the bank on Friday, and now there's another $80 missing from the deposit.

Are . . . you . . . kidding . . . me . . . I was so angry!

I was livid because someone was playing games. To make matters worse, we didn't understand how the heck that could happen because Jewel and I were the only two people with the key to the safe. I was fuming! This was not right!

Jewel was dropping the ball. What the hell! But despite my anger, I believed Jewel couldn't have been involved.

I simply couldn't accept that she had anything to do with it. She was a single mom that couldn't afford to lose her job. And because money transactions were the assistant manager's responsibility, I knew that the minute I told Rae money was missing, Jewel would get fired.

That afternoon, I went to Rae's office and told her the entire story. Naturally she was upset that I didn't come to her sooner. I would've been mad too; it didn't look good that I went to the managers retreat and didn't say anything. After I finished laying out the details, just as expected, the first words she uttered was, "You have to let Jewel go." But I stuck up for Jewel and told Rae I didn't believe she took it.

So, Rae said, "Ok, do you think she'd be willing to take a lie detector test?" I said yes. Then she asked if I'd be willing to take one, and I said, "Of course!"

I didn't know it yet, but that conversation was the start of everything going wrong in my career. The most treacherous year of my life was about to begin, the year I forgot I turned thirty. Remember the prayer I had in chapter 13? I told God, "*This is You! Not me! If I'm not supposed to be in this industry, pull me out because I won't!*"

Well let's just say it wasn't smart of me to talk to God that way. He didn't just pull me out; He dragged me out. That year became one of the darkest moments in my adult life. It was almost as if God made sure I knew I wasn't in control of the situation. He made it clear to me that I would not be able to return to property management. Ever!

BETRAYAL OF ALL SHAPES AND SIZES

When I returned to my office that day, I talked to Jewel and explained to her the severity of the situation. I told her she'd have to take a lie detector test and she agreed, as I knew she would. However, something changed that day.

Jewel stopped talking to me.

I wondered why, but it wasn't until the following two meetings with Rae that I understood.

In one of those meetings, it was noted that there were two other properties with the same machines, Gail's and Melanie's. They'd been working for Rae for nearly two decades at that point. Plus, they were Rae's best friends. Those three did everything together.

Rae called the three of us to her office one day and explained her role with the laundry machines. She reached in her desk drawer and pulled out a set of instructions and keys, telling us that she dropped the ball. Apparently, when the machines were installed, six years earlier, there was a series of reconciliations that was supposed to be happening. And Rae didn't do any of them.

Evidently, at the end of each month, Rae was supposed to go to each property and complete her own inspection, signing off that the totals were being calculated correctly. Then, the headquarters' accounting team was supposed to ensure that all the checks and balances were complete.

None of that was happening.

In fact, Rae showed us that the envelopes were still sealed. She never opened them or conducted one inspection of the machines after they were installed. Before we left, she told the three of us to conduct a detailed audit of all the money that was emptied dating back to day one. During my audit, I started to see a massive discrepancy dating back to when they were first installed, nearly three years before I got there.

Just then, Gail called me in a panic because her numbers were off by over $13,000.

She was shocked and scared. She said she didn't know what to do because unlike me, she was there the day the machine was installed. She sounded very concerned. I tried to console her, so I shared with her that my number was off by $19,000.

Wait, $19,000! What? Yup!

The next day, the three of us met at Rae's office to go over our audit. Of course, I was the first one to present my report. The room shook when I told them that the totals were off by $19,000. What was fascinating was the lack of empathy when I shared that many discrepancies happened before I started managing the property. The looks of judgement were so piercing, it penetrated my being at another level. If you thought that was bad, just wait. Next up was Gail. She presented her report and was proud to announce to the room that she was off by a few pennies.

A few pennies??? Really?

Just the day before she called me in a panic because she was off by over $13,000 and now that discrepancy was magically gone. Her words were incomprehensible to me. Just then, Rae ripped into me asking me how I was the only person in the room whose report showed a massive amount of theft. I could have thrown Gail under the bus, but I didn't. Instead, I sat there and took the betrayal, the judgement, the treachery. It was horrifying.

I looked at Gail with a void on my face. We both knew what was happening in the room that day. The only difference, and a big one at that, was that she was the boss's BFF, and I was an outsider. The next few weeks, back at the property, Jewel didn't make eye contact with me at all anymore. Whenever her cell phone rang, she ran outside to take the call. I wondered who she was speaking to, but it wasn't any of my business anyway, so I never asked.

Then one day, her phone rang. Like always, she ran outside to answer it. That day she was gone for a really long time. Residents were coming in and prospects as well to look at apartments. I didn't like what was happening because at the end of the day, she was still at work and had a job to do.

I got up to go find her, and it just so happened that as I was walking out, she was walking in. Just before we ran into each other, I heard her say, "Ok I will. Thanks Rae."

Rae??? Are you serious? What the hell was all that about?

I'd been doing this for over a decade and never seen a regional manager communicate privately with any position below a property manager, especially private cell phone conversations. Regional Manager's don't normally give their personal numbers to people.

Wow! Here we go again. The set-up was being arranged.

Don't get me wrong; I don't believe Rae intentionally set me up. Or maybe she did? I don't know. But what I do know is she decided that I was the bad guy in all this.

Now that the stage was set, Jewel and I took the lie detector test.

She passed hers, like I knew she would. Mine, on the other hand, was inconclusive.

Inconclusive? That's remarkable. The operator told me the test showed that I did not steal anything, as it should have because I didn't. I never stole a dime from any company I worked for. The part that was inconclusive was the 1/1000 chance I could have known who did. One in 1000? Ok? I guess? But as the property manager, wasn't it my job to speculate who did it? Wasn't it my job to investigate so that I can find out who did it?

Of course, I had thoughts of who would steal from the company! What manager wouldn't.

Nonetheless, the test showing I didn't steal anything wasn't good enough apparently. And the 1/1000 chance I assumed who did was good enough to paint the picture that I planned the whole thing. The sheer fact that Rae had known me before I was of legal age to even have a drink didn't mean anything to her. She knew the type of person I was, my work ethic, my honesty, my character. She knew very well I didn't steal from the company. But whatever! Just get it over with already, Rae!

15

CHANGE

TIME TO GO

A few days later, like any other day, I got up early, got ready, and went to work. Before I walked in the building, I sat in my car and prayed. After I finished praying, I sensed that I was going to be fired that day. As I was getting out of my car, I had a flash back of the violent prayer I made years earlier about my career. Everything about what had just happened re-played in my mind, re-playing in slow motion.

It was so slow that all the details were seared into my mind. The day I said goodbye to my career arrived. But even though I knew what was coming, that day, I felt a peace beyond all understanding.

Sure, I felt betrayed by someone I looked up to, but I couldn't blame her.

I told God in a direct way to remove me if I wasn't supposed to be there, and He did.

It wasn't the way I wanted it to happen, but I felt like God made it crystal clear that the door of property management was forever closed for me.

As I walked across the parking lot to the office, I slowly took in what the morning felt like. The breeze outside was cool, and the sun was bright and warm. I could feel the heat hugging my skin. There were flowers, freshly planted just outside the office, and the new fall-colored flags I ordered I could tell were installed that morning. I could hear the crispness of the flags clapping in the breeze.

When I walked inside, I put my things down. I was the only one there, so I immediately cleared out a box to put my belongings in. Then I sat at my desk and wrote a letter to Rae, the HR director, and the owners to rebut my termination. I don't remember the details I wrote in that letter, but I didn't hold much back. I certainly didn't agree with the fate Rae chose for me, but I understood the position I put her in.

Less than an hour later, Rae walked into my office. She sat in the chair in front of me and picked up the phone to call the HR director. She let the director do all the talking. The director began discussing the details, being extra careful to explain all the reasons why letting me go was the right thing to do. At the end of the one-way conversation, I told them that I emailed a rebuttal letter to the four owners of the company.

The HR director sounded nervous when I told her that.

She insisted on talking about the letter, saying, "Rebuttal letter? What rebuttal letter? What does it say? What did you put in it? Let's talk about that." I told her, "Why would I talk now? The decision has already been made right? I cc'd both of you in the email. You can read it yourself and see what it says."

The director said, "OK," then asked Rae if she needed anything else. Rae said no. She hung up the phone. That's when Rae looked up at me, and I saw her lips beginning to move. "Priscilla, I'm sorry it had to…"

"Stop! Rae, stop!" I said,

"We both know what's happening here. I'm not the only one that dropped the ball, but we both know that someone has to take the fall, and clearly that person is me." The way I was feeling that morning, I couldn't conceive hearing anything she had to say to me. She looked away from me, I grabbed my things, and left. Outside, my team was waiting. I hugged each one of them and said goodbye.

Did you catch what I said at the start of this chapter? Probably not.

Want to hear something fascinating? I bet you do. If you didn't notice, I said I was alone in the office that morning. Jewel must have known before I did what was going to happen because she never came in. My team messaged me later that day to tell me that she showed up immediately after I was terminated.

Wasn't that convenient!?!

That was the ultimate slap in the face from someone I was determined to save a job for and valued so much as a person, and as a friend.

THE LESSONS I LEARNED

In the rebuttal email I sent, I asked for a copy of my employee file. Days later, when I received it, what stuck out the most was what I saw at the very top of the package. It was an email sent from Rae to the HR director that read (I'm paraphrasing here), *"Please also add that Priscilla hired her niece's husband without my knowledge. I had no idea Liam was related to her."* First, Liam was not my niece's husband. And secondly, she knew very well who he was and approved of the hire. The only mistake I made was not getting the approval in writing.

Dragging my character in the dirt, that was uncalled for Rae!

For years after this dramatic ending to my career, I wondered what I would do if I ever saw Rae again. I was so incredibly bitter and mad. I hated her. I hated her for a very long time. Sure, I dealt with other supervisors that acted like that and did unspeakable things. But for some reason, the experience with Rae damaged me the most.

I recognized that for me to be successful in the next stage of my life, I had to learn how to forgive Rae.

I remembered hearing a sermon somewhere once where the pastor said that the best way to forgive those who have hurt you is to pray for them whenever their name enters your mind. So, I tried it. For years I prayed for Rae, a lot. It was a slow process but believe it or not, it worked.

Little by little, I grew to love her again. I started missing our conversations. I missed hearing the advice she gave. She always did give good counsel. Eventually, I wasn't scared of seeing her anymore.

Today, I'm incredibly thankful that God worked in my heart and showed me how to forgive. Because when the day came to see Rae again, I was ready. It was one of those encounters you can't run away from. We were at church; I was walking out of the building, and she was walking in. As soon as we locked eyes, I smiled and said, "Rae! Hi! How are you? It's good to see you." She couldn't look at me. She put her head down and gave me the lamest wave I ever seen. My youngest daughter Deja was with me and said, "Mom why are you saying hi to that lady? Clearly, she doesn't want to talk to you."

I told her, "Well honey, sometimes you have to be the bigger person and do the right thing anyway."

It's interesting how even kids can recognize telling human behaviors. I can write a whole other book just to talk about the lessons I learned in my first career. But I'll save you the trouble and summarize it. The main lesson I learned was to protect myself. I can still love people, but I learned to love them without sacrificing who I am. I learned to never change who I am for any human being. If I'm going to change, let it be for Jesus.

On the other hand, the lesson I learned from Rae was a heartfelt one. Heartfelt? You're probably thinking, *Wait a minute. Wasn't she ruthless to you?* In her own way, yes. Perhaps, because I've forgiven her, I don't see her as that anymore. At the end of the day, I believe people act the way they do because of the experiences they've had in their lives. Remember when I said, "Our memories underline our story, then our story underlines our thoughts, and those thoughts are what develops the why behind who we become." Don't forget, I looked up to Rae my entire adult life. For it to have ended the way it did with her hurt immensely.

She was more than a role model to me. She was an inspiration, a trusted friend. She was someone I looked up to and aspired to be like. I don't blame Rae for making the decision she made. I don't agree with how she went about it, but I also was not innocent in the situation either. I never stole from the company, but I delayed telling her about what happened. Even though my intentions were pure, it still was not the right decision to make. And I accept full responsibility for that.

In the end, a quote I read from my business mentor and the creator of the 10X movement, Grant Cardone rings true to me, and perhaps it can ring true for you too. Grant says, "Never take the position that things just happen to you; rather, they happen because of something you did or did not do."[1] The opportunities and experiences I had in my first career, although rewarding, also came at a high cost. I was broken as a child and when I started at eighteen, I buried my self-worth in my newfound career. I believe that's the reason I was so incredibly affected by my exit.

To me, it felt like I was losing my self-worth all over again. It was devastating!

In hindsight, I am exceedingly thankful for the things I learned being in that industry.

I literally grew up *within* my first career. All the lessons I learned while being in it allowed me to thrive in the next chapter of my story. And for that, I am grateful.

THE START OF SOMETHING NEW

So, what's next? I had no idea. I was in a whole new arena of life. All I knew since the age of eighteen was one thing. That was property management, and now it was gone. I don't have a degree, which disqualified me from the type of career that paid the same amount of money I was used to making.

Because of that, I was forced to do some soul-searching.

After months of submitting job applications. I began to pray and ask God to help me find my purpose again. This time, instead of doing things my way, I wanted it to be His idea, not mine.

Subconsciously, since I had the free time, I started doing nail art on myself. My nieces and some friends picked up on it, and they asked me to do their nails too. It was only gel polish, so I thought why not. I was having fun with it. A year passed; I ran into my old high school principal's secretary. I used to sit in her office and chat during my government class. She asked me if I still liked nails. I was really confused by the question at first. Then she told me, "Yea! You don't remember? I had my nails done all the time, and you used to love coming to my office to talk about nails." Hmm, really?

Shortly after that conversation, a friend of mine told me that I should seriously consider doing nails professionally. It was the first time I considered the idea. That evening, when my husband came home, I told him I needed to talk to him about something.

"Babe, I have something to tell you." Just then, he stopped me and said, "Wait before you say anything, on the way home I was thinking maybe you should consider getting your license to do nails."

What? I was shocked! How did he know? He had no idea what I was thinking about that day. And if you haven't noticed by now, I don't believe in coincidences. Like so many other times in my life, it had to be a God thing; there's no other explanation. None! You can't make stuff like that up. It's impossible. Embarking on this new journey was scary. But maybe, just maybe, I can change the trajectory of my life. I didn't want to be afraid of my future anymore. Surely, there must be something I can offer people.

What do I bring to society? Can I change my reality? Do I have the power to change my life? Can I endure what life throws my way? Can I find a better way to live? To thrive. Maybe this time I could teach myself to be the role model, the inspiration, the trusted friend I longed for others to be for me.

THE BEGINNING OF A COSMIC JOURNEY

In the coming weeks, I started to look at different beauty schools to attend. I stopped on one and made the decision to go for it. I didn't have the money to pay for tuition, so I maxed out one of my credit cards to enroll.

The day I picked up an acrylic brush, I knew I made the right decision.

Growing up, I watched my dad fix cars. He showed me how to use the reflection of the sun hitting the car to find waves on the surface of the repair. He taught me how to sand down a Bondo patch. He showed me how to use my fingers to create shadows and expose uneven spots. The first acrylic set of nails I did, I applied all those principles; it just made sense. To me, I was working on a tiny fender. I loved it!

The instructors at the beauty school were shocked when I told them I never did acrylic nails before. The entire process of the industry was new to me. I didn't know what to expect, so I went with the flow. It wasn't until after I graduated that I realized how hard it would be to become successful doing nails. As soon as I was out in the real world, I was competition. The nail techs I reached out to wanted nothing to do with me. I learned quickly that I was on my own.

16

MY PURPOSE STARTED TO UNFOLD

WALKING THROUGH IT

Even though I was on my own, I wasn't deterred. I mean, why would I be? After all the lessons I learned in my last career, why would this be any different? I embarked on a new journey, and I needed to see myself through it. Just like before, the only difference was I was in control of my future now. I'm sure you've heard this before but believe me, it's true. I'm living proof.

We grow through our difficulties, because it's the process of walking "*through*" a difficulty that we find ourselves.

If you look at the word *through*, what does it mean? Now, all I ask is that you hear me out. Read this definition slowly. Try to paint a picture of this in your mind; I promise it'll make sense. The word *through* is used as a function word to indicate a period of time or completion.[1]

This is fascinating! Think about how you feel when you're walking *through* difficulties. Can you feel it? OK! Seemingly, it could be that the difficulties you go *through* are nothing more than continuations of time that lead you toward the completion of a process or a period in your life. The difficulty happens just before the completion.

Now let's look at the words process and period, what do they mean?

1. The definition of process is—a natural phenomenon marked by gradual changes that lead toward a particular result.[2]
2. The definition of period is—the completion of a cycle, a series of events, or a single action.[3]

In other words, your difficulties are means to an end. It's a series of functions that indicate the completion of, I believe, your purpose. It's all about the completion. It's the gradual changes during your difficulties that lead toward the completion of that cycle you are in. If that didn't make sense to you, please go back and read it again, slowly. It's imperative that you understand what I'm describing here. Did you get it? Good, now that it's clear.

Perhaps looking at difficulties in this way will help you understand where you are today in your season of life. I'm not saying difficulties are easy; they're never easy. But if you endure it, be patient with it. Walk through it. I promise you it'll be worth it. It's been worth it for me, which is why I'm glad I chose the beauty industry and chose to do nails. In fact, so many people think that you can't possibly make a living doing nails.

They're wrong! I know nail techs who are successful and are easily making a six-figure income. To achieve that, you may think that you need to have a high-level business degree. You don't! But you do need tenacity, work ethic, patience, courage, and determination.

Knowing what the beauty industry can do for people is important. But understanding how the beauty industry can impact suffering young women is vital.

Many of you reading this book, I'm certain, have been to a salon before. Have you ever stopped to think how you, as the client, are helping the person that is servicing you? I'm not talking about money. In fact, it's not about the money at all.

You see, the salon isn't just a workplace. This industry is a mental health-developing, therapeutically rich atmosphere consumers don't even know exist. The young women that pursue this space as a career are subconsciously creative people. That's true, but there's something you don't know about them. Many of them have secret lives they wouldn't dare share with you or others. Some are living in abusive relationships, broken homes, and/or are struggling with addiction. Perhaps they are even recovering from being trafficked. They're lost, broken, and desperately needing someone to simply see them, someone to meet them in their situation and accept them for who they are, no matter how broken they are.

For others, this career is the last option for them to change their situation. Whatever it may be, because of their life experiences, these young women think and act differently than the average person. The trauma of feeling different can be extremely lonely. The way they isolate themselves is misunderstood, and, by many, is interpreted as insecure or insincere, perhaps even deceitful. It's judgements like these that leave them confused about their identities, who they are and how they fit in.

You know by now that the young women I just described used to be me.

I lived the secret life that I never shared with anyone, not even my kids or my husband.

I was the young woman that was lost, broken, and desperately needing someone to meet me in my situation. I couldn't afford beauty school, but I went into debt anyway because this industry was my last resort. Working as a nail tech and holding clients' hands as I worked in my creative space, I never felt so free. I learned I was good at something that brought me genuine joy.

My clients had no idea that their acceptance of who I was and who I was working so hard to become was quite literally saving my life. Their compliments encouraged me. Their appreciation for a service well done began to thaw my cold heart and reminded me that I wasn't isolated, lonely, and judged anymore. For once, I could be myself.

THERE'S SOMETHING ABOUT BEAUTY PEOPLE RARELY SEE

After being in this industry for a decade, what I found was not everyone in a salon or beauty school was reaping the benefits of this industry like I was, so I started studying why. And through my research, I discovered something. I found that there is a system to beauty schools' people don't talk about. Perhaps it's because they don't know, or maybe they do, but I guess keeping it out of sight and out of mind is a better way to process the sick reality of our world. Nevertheless, I believe this system should be shouted about from the rooftops everywhere because of the impact it can have in our community.

Did you know that you can attend beauty school and start the process of obtaining a license at sixteen years old? I didn't.

Why are people not talking about this? I wish I had started in this industry when I was seventeen. It never even crossed my mind. And like I told you earlier, it was obvious I liked nails because I talked about it all the time with the principal's secretary at my old high school. I went to salons to get my nails done, but no one ever talked to me about the opportunities this industry provided. Imagine for a minute if I had started back then, if someone came alongside me and showed me what to do and how to do it. I would have found a way to escape the dangerous lifestyle I was in. An opportunity like this, no doubt, would have changed the trajectory of my life.

There are thousands of young adults, young women, that age out of the foster care system every year in this country. Not to mention there are young women everywhere being trafficked. Then there are those living lifestyles they hate but are stuck in it. They're told by their assailer that no one will love them after knowing the things they've done. They're reminded daily that they're damaged, and they have no hope of becoming something more than the environment they're in. These young women believe they don't have a way to escape, and yet these women have no idea that this industry can save them from mayhem.

So far, I've learned that if the beauty world could do this for me, how can I pay it forward?

Keep reading, because by the time you finish this book, you will never look at salons the same way again.

EDUCATION

Before I share anything on this, let me just say that through my research, what I found is not a reflection of all the beauty schools. There are amazing beauty schools in New Mexico and in the U.S. alike. However, the number of remarkable beauty schools are extremely small. The research I did didn't just cover my state; I also researched other states before coming to my conclusion.

What you will read here is what I've discovered in nearly a decade of research. The way I see it is if we're going to impact lives and give young women safe environments to thrive in, first we need to address the issues within our beauty schools. I'll start by asking you a question, in hopes that in the end, this will all make sense. Have you ever seen something or heard something that piqued your interest? It could be anything.

What's the first thing you do? You Google it or look it up on YouTube to learn more about it. We all do it, don't you? I know I do. In the beginning of anything we do in life, we have to rely on someone else to give us the information because we have no idea how to do it yet.

It's the same thing with your career.

1. First, there are parts of a job that you only see.
2. Then, there are parts of it that you hear about but never experience until you're in it for a while, or you'll experience it after you've been promoted, perhaps.
3. Finally, there are parts that hide behind the scenes. Like the processes and the awareness of what makes the job tick, you know, the secret sauce. The how of how it works, and what makes it sell.

The truth is, you don't know what you don't know, so how can you look for things you don't know exist? Here's an example of something you don't know about beauty schools. We've already established that there's a lack of awareness in that the beauty industry can help young people escape their harsh realities. For this next part, I'm going to rest on the nail industry for a moment. Not because the other parts of the business aren't important, but that's where I have the most experience in because I'm a nail tech.

The top schools I researched that have amazing programs for their students do not offer a nail program. I've found that sometimes it's because they don't want to, since nail programs have the least expensive tuition costs. Other times it's because they can't find instructors.

This is a big problem! Let me explain. In the U.S., depending where you live:

1. The nail technology program takes anywhere from 350-600 hours to complete. That equates to a student being able to start working within four to six months.
2. When a nail tech wants to attend a top school, they are forced to pay tuition for the full cosmetology program. In some states, that program can take up to 2300 hours to complete. That not only doubles a nail tech's tuition rate, but it can sometimes triple it, depending on where they live. And it can take up to two years to complete the course versus six months.

3. Not to mention, in the cosmetology program, nail techs only get about two weeks of training on nails, a few weeks of training on skin, and the rest of the training is on hair.

This is public information that can be found on school websites and the Board of Cosmetology website for the state you live in. All course curriculum schools offer lists the hours calculated for each portion of the program, which in my opinion, based on what I've found, nail programs are often treated like the red headed stepchild of the beauty industry.

How can students succeed with odds like that? It's no wonder many nail techs don't survive their first year in this career. In addition to everything I said above, the schools that do offer a nail program, most often than not, have instructors that are *not* nail techs themselves.

How do you teach a trade when you're not in it?

I've seen school directors guarantee students that they will make so much money just by offering the same client multiple services. The only problem with this philosophy is who in their right mind will spend up to $600 to stay in a salon all day long getting their hair done, nails done, facial, and hair removal done by the same person?? That's absurd! And it almost never happens. I've seen instructors tell students that they'll immediately become entrepreneurs and never have to work for anyone after they graduate. Except what they fail to mention are the steps the student must take before they can work on their own and be successful doing it. The amount of work it takes to become an entrepreneur, let alone the knowledge it takes to build a profitable business, is hard!

When I was in beauty school, I didn't learn much about the business side of this industry. I had to spend thousands of dollars to learn every-thing I know today on how to grow and be successful. I was fortunate enough to have prior experience running someone else's business assets, but not everyone was given that option or experience.

Now, be patient. I understand many of you aren't nail techs or even in the beauty industry. But keep reading; I will bring this full circle.

BE THE CHANGE

Knowing what I know today about the beauty industry, who would I be if I didn't attempt to solve these problems? The incredible thing about walking through my difficulties is that I learned how to persevere.

Now, when I'm faced with a problem, I become more resilient and determined to solve it, determined to make an impact.

Remember the purpose I told you about that I found when I was fourteen, but I ran from it? Well, this industry stopped me dead in my tracks. I saw the decline our society was going in. The respect for human dignity was becoming scarce.

I'm about to open a door to my journey that I never shared with anyone.

The things that I have seen while being on this journey I cannot unsee, which is why, now, I have an unwavering desire to change the culture of the beauty industry. And this book is where I am going to outline exactly how I'm going to do it. Are you ready? I hope you are. Because it's happening.

17
THIS IS NOT JUST A SALON

MY PATH TO PAIXXÃO

Paixxão.Co is my company; it's a safe space I created where everyone can be themselves and be given the opportunity to grow. Unbeknownst to me, my path to Paixxão began over twenty years ago when I went to a local nail salon to get a pedicure. What I did not realize was, that day would be the day that I left with something that would forever change the way I looked at salons. For the next two years, I battled with a terrible toenail fungus. It was so bad that I had to take a very strong medicine to kill it. I had to run tests on my kidney before, during, and after the treatment of my toenail fungus.

My toenail healed on the third year, but then that little pesky bacterium came back. My doctor told me that it would be best if I removed my toenail and apply medicine for it to never grow back. That was not an option for me, so I did everything I could to get rid of the infection. The experience traumatized me! Till this day, I do not walk barefoot anywhere; I even wear flip-flops in my own shower. Yea, I know that sounds ridiculous, but the trauma was so overwhelming that now I can't shake it. It's in my head.

Over a decade later, I'm in beauty school. When I graduated, I had a hard time finding a salon to work at. I wanted to be near other nail techs to learn from them, except that environment didn't exist. And the nail techs I reached out to, like I told you before, wanted nothing to do with me because I was competition. Why would they share their knowledge with someone else? They automatically assumed I would steal all their clients. I ended up renting a small space in the corner of a small hair salon. The owner of the salon was a veteran nail tech of thirty years, Angel. She worked alongside Danny Haile, an internationally recognized nail tech and founder of EZ Flow Nail Systems, and now Gelish, the first brush-in-bottle gel polish ever invented.

Angel was a good mentor when it came to encouraging me to push through the hard times of the business, but she kept her distance. She allowed me to grow on my own. She gave me advice, then stepped back. Sometimes I wish she would have taken me under her wings and mentored me one on one. We could have been a great team.

For weeks, I passed out fliers all over town with pictures of my work. Then I started a Groupon deal. Each service took me at least three hours to do, and Groupon was paying me $15 for each deal. That's $5 an hour and nearly 90% less than what I was making as a property manager.

MY PROMISE TO GOD

Despite the low salary, I prayed and told God that I wanted to start tithing 10% of my income. My parents always said God did more with 90% than the 100% people tried to keep, but how could I tell Danny that I was going to donate 10% of what was already a massive pay cut? He'd kill me! So, I prayed about it again and said,

> "Father, I know You can do exceedingly and beyond
>   with 90% than what I could ever do with 100% of
>   my income. You brought me this far. The only way
>   I believe that I can tithe is by using the cash that I
>   collect from tips. That way Danny doesn't see the

money hit the bank and feel like it's another bill we have to pay. Lord, I pray that the cash is enough. You know my heart, and You know what plans You have for me and my business."

You wouldn't believe what happened after that. I was dumbfounded when I started to see that every single month after that prayer, for at least two years, the cash I collected was exactly 10% of my income.

TO THE PENNY!

That's when I knew that I knew that I knew I was walking in my purpose. Whatever that walk looked like, I had to be willing to push *through* the difficulties.

PURE

After I left Angel's salon, I opened a small studio with another girl I met in beauty school. I was so excited to start my official first company, Pure. It was there that I began to meticulously design and create my Signature Hot Towel Pedicure everyone knows me for today. Unfortunately, that company suffered a nightmare ending. The vision I had of what Paixxão is now, I had from the very beginning of partnering with this person. Her name was Raegan. We spent countless hours designing a beautiful space. We agreed I'd do nails, and she would do facials. It was perfect!

However, as soon as we opened the doors, I rarely saw Raegan. In the nearly two years the business was open, I saw her maybe a handful of times. She had clients come to their appointments, and she wouldn't show up. I was so embarrassed.

Once the negative reviews began to pour in, I knew that the business wouldn't last. I couldn't be a reflection of that. So, I told her I wanted out. Let's just say the business divorce was horrendous. Any suggestion I made to dissolve the partnership was confronted with massive amounts of hostility. In the end, I came to work one day to find my business ransacked. Everything was cleared out, except the supplies I used to work. All the pretty furniture, rugs, pillows, and decorations we both invested in were taken. Oh! Even the logo was stripped off the window.

Despite the juvenile ending, my clientele was growing. I decided that I was going to move out of that space and find my own. When I told Danny I wanted to open my own salon, he cringed at the idea. How could I blame him? He had a first-row seat to what just happened with my business partner. My income was slowly increasing but starting a new company? We both knew it would be expensive. We agreed on a monthly rent budget. Let's just say it was really low, so low that for months, I was being laughed out of tours with real estate agents.

PASSION

Before I started looking for a space to rent, first I had to find a name for my new business. The first word that came to mind was Passion. For days, I played around with different logos using the word. Nothing was catching my eye though. Then I thought, *Duh, pick a Portuguese word; you're Brazilian.*

I stumbled across the Portuguese word Paixão. Right away, I loved the way it looked. It was sexy!

I couldn't remember what the word meant so I took a screenshot of it and texted it to my sister Eklesia. I asked her if she recognized it and asked her what it meant. She said, "Oh yea! I know that word. It looks cool. It means passion." No way! Seriously? I thought, *Wow, what are the odds?*

Next, I called the owner of the beauty school I graduated from. He was kind enough to let me go to the school to meet the nail techs that were in the program at the time. I introduced myself to the class and told them that I was opening a nail salon, and my vision was to only hire aspiring nail techs fresh out of school. I told them I'd train them and teach them how to become successful nail techs. There were a few girls there that were all in, except when they asked me where the salon was going to be, I told them I didn't have a space yet, but I assured them that they could trust me. And they did. For months they got ridiculed at school because they were trusting a stranger with the fate of their careers.

That's when I started to pray. Deep down, I knew this new journey for me was a God thing. I felt it! I had no idea what would happen, especially how it was going to happen, but I knew that starting this company was the right thing to do. I was having such a hard time finding a space to rent, so I prayed harder.

> "Lord, what is happening? I know I have a purpose, you showed it to me when I was young and now I'm here, trying to grasp this purpose and I don't have the money to start another company and I don't want to put any more pressure on my marriage. Please find me a space. In that space, I need enough room for at least four nail stations, one hair station, one room for waxing, a waiting room for the clients, and a place for a break room and laundry room."

The week after, I reluctantly scheduled a tour with a married couple that were both real estate agents to look at a location in midtown Albuquerque. To be honest, I didn't want to be in that part of town, but I went anyway. The suites I was looking at were not working at all. Just then, the lady agent told me, "You know what? There's a space downstairs that I think would work great for a salon." Downstairs? I had no clue there even was such a thing. All the years I lived in Albuquerque, I drove by the building hundreds of times and never knew there were suites underground. Nonetheless, we walked down the stairs. When she opened the front door, I thought.

Holy moly!!! I stood back and just took in the moment. It was perfect!

· · ·

In a split second, I was able to envision Paixxão.

Everything I asked for in my prayer was there. Everything! It was all accounted for. Wow!

I was amazed. But, now for the hard part. My budget. I told the agent, "OK, I love the space. I want to lease it, but my budget is extremely low. So low that I've been laughed out of places left and right." The gentlemen agent said, "OK, let's hear it!" When I told him the number, he paused. It was the longest fifteen seconds of my life. Then he said, "I think we can make that work." WHAT!!! REALLY??? I was forever grateful.

For the next six months, during the day I serviced my clients, and, in the evening, I was doing construction on the new location. I hired an old contractor friend to move a couple of walls. Everything else I did myself. I built the platforms for the pedicure stations; I painted; I took down doors and filled in holes in the walls; I installed shelves and stripped floors. It was a lot of work. But I had to finish it as fast as I could because two more girls reached out to me for a job. Now I had a team of four people all patiently waiting for me to train them. One of them graduated early so she jumped on board and started helping me set up the salon.

Finally, in 2016 Paixxão opened!

I had a meeting with the team just before we opened the doors. I told them, "OK ladies! Paixxão is open for business. Here's what's going to happen: we are going to open those doors; we are going to blow up; we're going to get the Best of the City award; and when we get that, we will expand." Little did I know that everything I said in that meeting happened in less than a year. Now what?

For an entire year, I didn't collect a dime in pay. I was servicing clients, but all my income went to paying the bills and paying my team. Danny was getting frustrated because my income was non-existent. I tried my best to assure him that the sacrifice would pay off. I knew it would; I just couldn't explain how. I was walking by faith, and that was all I could say to him at the time. After we found out we were named "Best Nail Salon in Albuquerque," I went home and told Danny I had to expand the salon.

His response was expected. "Have you lost your mind? How the hell are you going to do that? You can't even pay yourself anything now!"

I said, "I know, babe, but you don't understand. I told the girls that we would expand once we got awarded with the Best of the City award. Who would I be if I don't stick by what I said?"

"I don't care!" he said, "They aren't the ones paying for all of this."

"I know," I said. "I will figure out how I'm going to do this. Just be patient with me." He rolled his eyes and walked away. I asked myself repeatedly if I was making the right decision.

Think about this for a moment. I was putting my marriage on the line for four ladies I barely knew. Who does that? And why would anyone do that? See, for me create a safe space my team could thrive in, first I had to build up my own career. I did this by picking up a gig delivering newspapers in the wee hours of the night. That meant I worked 18-hour plus days. Seven days a week I got up between 2-4am. On school days, after delivering papers, I'd get home around 6am, get the kids ready for school, then I went to the salon and did nails till 9pm. Sometimes later. Unfortunately, after years of working like this I damaged my neck pretty bad. I had five disks that were bulging, causing me to be in excruciating pain. I kept my pain silent for a long time because I was determined to make Paixxão work. I was determined to change the culture of nail salons for aspiring nail techs. Sadly, for me, because of the injuries I caused I was never able to become the nail tech I knew I could be. That's when I decided to show others how they could obtain the success I never could.

I loved those girls like they were my own children. I wanted so badly to see them succeed. That was the moment I realized that this wasn't just a salon for me; I was changing lives. I was becoming their Rae, and I refused to let them down. All I cared about was that I was given the opportunity to pour into my team and show them that someone was in their corner and willing to share information that will help their success and confidence.

I was not afraid to teach them everything I knew about the business and all the lessons I learned along the way. I taught them more than just how to do nails, I taught them that it was ok to make mistakes and encouraged them to do better, both in their careers and their personal lives. I became mom. I gave them parenting advice, dating advice. I was there when things were falling apart, and they needed a shoulder to cry on. I cried with them when tragedy struck, I laughed with them when someone did something silly. It was awesome.

18

NEW BEGINNINGS

TOO BIG TOO SOON?

Within weeks of the daunting conversation I had with my husband, I signed a lease for the space next door. I made several trips to local beauty schools. I introduced myself and talked to the students about my salon. I told them the story, explained my vision, and told them that I was expanding and would be looking to hire several nail techs. Within a few weeks, I had commitments from fourteen nail techs. Fourteen!

Within a few months, Paixxão went from being a small nail salon of four nail techs (five if you include me) to a massive nail salon of nineteen nail techs. I wasn't thinking about the consequences of growing so fast.

Honestly, I didn't know any better. I was a brand-new business owner. As the team grew, the drama started to grow too. Of course, when you have that many people under one roof, there will be disagreements: that's expected. The problem I didn't account for was the time and energy everyone needed from me. I was still servicing clients full time, but it was becoming exceedingly obvious that I could not handle all the pressure of being a mentor, trainer, and mom to everyone while still being behind the chair all day and being a wife and mom to my own three children.

The stress was weighing on me. My body started shutting down. Besides my neck, my back also started having issues. The muscle spasms from the stress were awful. I knew that eventually I'd have to give something up, and that something had to be my clients. But how can I stop seeing my clients? Everything they had done for me and my growth, from the support they gave me to the love they showed me to the confidence they gave me at a time I needed it the most. I felt like

---

I would be letting them down if I stopped doing their nails.

Not to mention the original team I started the company with started to feel as if our little family was breaking apart. I was trying! I promise I was trying my best to manage everything on my own, but I knew I needed help. But there was not one person willing to step up to help me with the business operations side of the company. I became the giver of all things but never the receiver.

Just then, the company I ordered my lotions and scrubs from for my Signature Hot Towel pedicures discontinued the product line. Ahh! Are you kidding me? I called them and asked them why they weren't going to make it anymore, and they said that it just wasn't selling fast enough. I bought whatever they had left and started searching for a new line. But nothing was working. So now what? I was going to have to figure this out. Changing my pedicures was not an option.

During all the staff issues, managing a massive business (bookkeeping, accounting, marketing, accounts receivables/payables, housekeeper, inventory manager, customer service manager), and still servicing clients, I somehow found time to learn how to make lotion and scrubs that required a special method in order to do my pedicures. Oh! How could I forget—clients started asking about private parties, so I expanded again, to the suite on the other end, and created a beautiful private event space for bridal parties. I know! I know! I was a psycho right. Connotation accepted!

Meanwhile, because all my attention was on operations, I didn't realize that a cabal was being formed.

My vision of changing the culture began to slip through my hands. It felt as if I was swimming against a strong current. I was trying my best to keep everything together, but eventually I started to sense something wasn't right. The salon family didn't feel the same anymore. I recognized I had some bad apples on the team, but I could not find the courage to let them go. I loved them too much!

Looking back now, maybe I did them a disservice by keeping them, not because they were bad people. They weren't always that way. I couldn't shake the thought that I turned them into bad apples because the time they needed me the most, I was pre-occupied with trying to run a business. A massive company at that. Besides having a large team to manage, the salon was also servicing over 1,000 clients on a monthly basis.

THE RESPECT

One year, on October 1st, I knew I lost the little respect I had left from my original team. If you don't know me personally, you wouldn't know this about me, but I hate Halloween. I never told anyone this story before. I must have been four or five years old, and we still lived in Brazil. My mom had to step out for some reason and left me and my sister home alone. Before my mom left, she told us not to answer the door to anyone, and especially not to accept any candy if it was offered.

It wasn't long after my mom left that there was a knock at the door. My sister ran to answer it. I begged her not to, but she didn't listen. When she opened the door, I saw a terrifying looking person standing there. Then they said, "Trick or Treat." My sister asked them, "What does that mean?" The person replied and said, "What kid doesn't know what trick or treat means? It means you give us candy. It's Halloween."

My sister told them we weren't allowed to celebrate Halloween. They were so shocked that they offered my sister a piece of candy. She took it and shut the door. I told with her not to eat it, but she did anyway, saying, "It's fine. It's just candy." She seemed fine for hours. My mom came home, and she got us ready for bed. Then, in the middle of the night, my sister woke up screaming. She was staring at the corner of the ceiling with complete fear in her eyes, repeatedly screaming, "It's right there; it's right there." I couldn't see anything, but I was so scared I started to scream too.

My mom ran into the room and began to ask us if we accepted candy from anyone while she was gone. My sister was still freaking out, in horror. Then I told my mom that she ate candy from someone that came to the door. As soon as I said that, my mom ran out of our room to her bedroom and grabbed her Bible. She immediately began to pray over my sister, claiming the blood of Jesus and yelling out Scripture over her.

Within minutes, she snapped out of it and fell lifeless.

My mom woke her up, then she prayed over us and told me everything was ok now. Till this day, I can't stand Halloween. I don't understand the celebration of ugly beings bringing so much value to death. And after the experience with my sister, I was not a fan. At all. I never felt like I had to tell people that story for them to understand why I dislike the holiday so much. I always assumed that those around me would have enough respect for me as a person to respect my decision and let it go.

I don't owe anyone an explanation as to why I dislike something. That is of course until I walked into my salon one year on October 1st. I was horrified by the hideous decorations EVERYWHERE. Seriously, you don't understand; it was obnoxious. It's as if the team wanted it to look ridiculous. I played it off cool, but I was horrified. The thoughts of what I experienced as a kid came rushing to my mind. All I could think of every time I walked inside my business was the look on my sister's face just before she fell lifeless on my mom's arms, the sheer terror she had in her eyes that night.

For thirty days, I had to re-live that moment. It was awful! I was so offended by the sheer disrespect. One thing I always talk about is respect; it's the thing I revere the most. When people lose respect, it's only a matter of time before things begin to fall apart. For thirty days, it was as if my wishes meant nothing to them anymore. They stopped caring about my thoughts and aspirations.

They stopped caring about what I was working so hard to build at Paixxão.

I know it's just decorations, but to me it was more than that. It was the loss of respect that scorched me.

EXODUS

The next several months, the cabal got stronger and stronger. I started hearing conversations about secret meetings. Clients were calling me left and right complaining about the language in the salon and the conversations the team was having among themselves in front of clients when I wasn't around. Many clients told me that they weren't going to be returning because the atmosphere was changing. Then the new team I hired started feeling the heaviness that was in the air too. In fact, many were coming to me and telling me how they were being disrespected by some of the team members.

There was one scenario in particular that didn't sit well with me at all. I learned that one of my techs was telling my brand-new nail techs that they had first dibs on any walk-ins that came in. And only if they didn't want the walk-in was when the new crew could take it. That is not right, at all! I never did that to them! Where and when did they think treating a brand-new nail tech like that was ok? I provided everything for them to succeed in their careers, but they weren't reciprocating the gift by simply being good team players.

All I asked was for them to return the favor and be role models for the next person. The culture I worked so hard to build was falling apart before my very eyes. Despite everything that was happening, I was still trying to stay positive. I was still talking to them about Paixxão growing. I still believed that everyone that called Paixxão home was being given a great opportunity. All the speeches I gave and encouragement I attempted to deliver weren't working though. It's as if the sense of opportunity suddenly turned to privilege then to resentment. How does that happen? Perhaps there's a fine line between opportunity and accountability. As a business owner you expect that the people that work in your company would respect it as much as you do but that doesn't always happen. I put my life, my marriage at risk for this, and I wasn't going to just let it slip through my hands like this.

So, instead I decided to pull back the reigns and start taking back control of my company.

I updated the business contract and had a meeting about the structures that were going to change. I had no other choice then to hold everyone accountable for the intentions they had with my company. See, people can have good hearts. They can be amazing human beings, but internal intentions speak louder than the outer shell they show others. Well, lo and behold, their true intensions showed itself, because within forty-eight hours, there was a mass exodus that happened. I was devastated! Not because they decided to leave but by the way they left.

Many of them posted a message on their social media accounts saying that their ethics and values no longer aligned with mine.

I believe with my whole heart that God heard the conversations I never could.

And I had to be ok with Him allowing this massive transition. I knew that I didn't have the heart to let any of them go, so they had to leave on their own and that's ok. Accepting that not everyone will share in our successes is hard, but it will make all the hard work worth it for those who want to be a part of it and need it the most.

I'm sure they have their own reasons for feeling the way they did. Before the exodus happened, nothing was brought to my attention about these ethics and values they posted about. If the conversation wasn't important enough to be had with me, then I'm not going to assume it was that important to them in the first place. It was an excuse to justify their actions.

How would I have known what they were thinking? I'm not a mind reader. Frankly, I was shocked to see the posts because ethics, values, as respect has always been a part of the demeanor I convey. But it's ok, to each their own. Just like I did for Rae, every time their names or faces popped into my head, I prayed them. In fact, I still do, till this day. Families fight, and sometimes families break up, but that doesn't mean the love goes away. I wish them all the best in life and in their careers. My hand was always open and willing to help them in their time of need. Sometimes that meant giving people pay advancements and paying their rent or car payments. Regardless of what happened, I wouldn't have changed a thing. Well, maybe one thing.

I would've been there for them more emotionally, perhaps had more one-on-ones with them and asked for their suggestions on how to help them through the transition of growing so fast. Other than that, I know I did my best with the hand I was dealt. I can't imagine that would be the first and last exodus. Change, whether it be planned or not can be a good thing.

In the end, the mission continued. The vision didn't die. I must continue to walk *through* the difficulties, because there's an entire world of young women out there that need a village of people willing to meet them where they are and offer them a hand to pull them out of their chaos.

IT ALL MADE SENSE

Less than two weeks following the exodus, the world shut down because of COVID-19. It's funny how things work out. After being shut down for over two months, we opened our doors again. What was interesting was that we had the exact number of nail techs that allowed us to social distance when we returned. Each person sat at alternating stations. I measured, and it was exactly six feet apart.

Can you believe it? Looking back now, if I still had a team of nineteen, there was no way everyone could return to work. There would be no room. How could I have chosen who returned and who didn't? Plus, how complicating would it have been to organize that schedule?

Wow! God's timing never ceases to amaze me.

When the *new* team returned to the salon, the culture I had visions of was operating in full force. Clients were loving the new atmosphere. What was crazy to me though was the feedback I started getting after the exodus. Clients were coming out of the woodwork telling me stories about the things that were happening behind my back. Dude! Why weren't you telling me this before?

Nonetheless, the business grew. I've since hired more people. I let some go, and I converted the event space to a hair salon. The team that remains now is an amazing group of young women, eager to learn and excited to grow. Many see the vision that I have for Paixxão and are happy to be a part of it.

Now when I hire people, they're accepted and surrounded by love and support. When I'm training, the team gathers around me and tells the new hires that if they have any questions to ask anyone, and they will help them. We've had team retreats and team pool parties. Some are joining exercise classes together. It's awe-inspiring to watch how the team has rallied together.

Some have received promotions to well-paying management roles. Paixxão, where it is today, is what I always dreamed, what I prayed for.

I love where we are right now, and I'm so eager to see where we will be in the future.

Don't get me wrong; yes, things are great. But like any other growing business, we still face challenges. There are still systems that we are working hard every day to implement. The difference this time though is that the blueprint is laid out for everyone to see. And it's simple enough to understand and see how the team fits in it. The only thing left for them to do is ask themselves, do I fit in? Am I aligned with this Mission? And do I want to work through the challenges to change the culture? Am I ok with being a part of a solution that is bigger than me? That requires me to be selfless and open to putting others above myself? For those that are honest with themselves and will openly answer these questions, little by little, are aligning with our Mission and helping Paixxão put in place a structure that will change many lives in Albuquerque and beyond.

19

THE BEST IS YET TO COME

THE WORLD STOPPED

I'll be honest; I didn't want to have a section about COVID. We hear about it so much already. But in all honesty, COVID-19 helped me shift my focus on the direction I wanted Paixxão to go in. After the shutdown, we were forced to operate at 25% for over a year. The salon grew in clientele during that time, but not by me hiring more people to work. It grew because of the sheer commitment my existing team made by making room to squeeze clients in wherever they could.

The elegant and hygienic alternative we're already known for attracted more clients to the salon. I pride myself on the sanitation process I implemented in the salon. Sterilizing tools and throwing away porous tools after each use became sought after by clients. COVID reminded people that sanitation is extremely important, especially in nail salons.

One thing I hated the most about COVID was seeing how it was impacting service providers. There were people that didn't qualify for assistance because they were considered self-employed. Salons were shutting their doors everywhere. It was heartbreaking to watch. Witnessing all of that made me look at my company from a different light, so much so that I made my next target finding other ways to support young women in the beauty industry. I started by having conversations with Danny about starting a nonprofit.

I didn't know what that would look like, much less how I would get it done. But one thing I did know for sure was the number of hurting women just got bigger. I heard stories on the news about ladies being beaten to death because their abusive spouses were home during the shutdown. Add the financial stress to that equation, and you have a disaster. I thought there must be a way to solve this problem. So, there I went, researching all about nonprofits, what types already existed, and how I can pay it forward to help these women.

Over the course of the next two years, miracles started to happen, doors began to swing open, and my focus started to move to something bigger than Paixxão, something bigger than me. If you don't believe me, just wait.

THE VISION

On October 4, 2020, I went to church. Nothing special, just a typical day. When I got there, I learned there was a guest speaker. Her name is Noel Yeattes, she's the president of World Help Foundation. She shared a video presentation on how we can make a difference and end sexual slavery happening around the world, especially in Thailand. She talked about the culture and explained how little girls as early as eight years old are being sold by their parents because they didn't have the means to provide for their families. The presentation touched me in a colossal way.

Then, one of the ladies from the worship team came on stage and started to sing a song by Lauren Daigle called "Rescue." Something happened to me during that song. As I listened to the lyrics, it talked about not being hidden or forgotten. It described how although people are broken, they are not hopeless. It depicted that although their innocence is being stolen, God hears their SOS. He will send an army to find them and rescue them.

Remember the story I told you about my dad at the start of this book? How he had a vision of Albuquerque, and how it was that vision that set into motion the next several years of his life?

Well . . . what I'm about to tell you is a lot like what happened to my dad.

During the song, out of nowhere, I felt a heavy burden being laid on my shoulders for those young ladies. Not just the ones from Thailand, but everywhere, especially in Albuquerque.

It felt like God grabbed me by the shirt and told me enough was enough.

You see, I was supposed to be like those little girls, yet God pulled me out. Although my innocence was stolen, God heard my SOS. He sent an army to find me and rescued me. The burden got stronger as it grew heavier and heavier, and I felt like God was yelling at me,

"I PULLED YOU OUT!"

Just then, I had a flash back of myself at thirteen. I saw my environment. I could smell it; I could hear the thoughts that were going through my head at that time. I was thirteen again. Standing there in church that day, with my eyes closed, as tears began to flow, I started to feel trapped again. I was surrounded by fear and confined in a tiny space in my head. I felt the burden of not being seen or heard all over again and was forced to confront my past in a very public way. I don't know how else to describe what happened next, other than it felt like an inner voice telling me,

"I've given you the resources to help but you are
hoarding it."

Then at that very second, my entire body went numb. I started crying profusely. For nearly thirty years I ran from the thirteen-year-old me yet there I was being her all over again. I never cried so hard in my life. The grunts were deafening. I sat down to try and compose myself. My arms and hands were tingling. I couldn't control anything. My son Nakqi grabbed my hand and was holding it tightly, not understanding what was happening to me.

My cry grew louder and louder. I couldn't control myself. I never groaned like that before. It was as if, just for a moment, God allowed me to feel what He felt for me when I was lost. What he feels for every girl stuck in those situations. The grief was intense. The sadness I felt at that moment was immeasurable. It was pure desolation, misery, and sorrow. While all of this is happening in the real world, my eyes were shut so tight, but I started to see an image play in my mind like a clip out of a movie.

I was floating in what felt like outer space, looking down. Surrounded by complete darkness. That's when I began to see the silhouette of a globe and quickly realized it was earth. Except at the same time the silhouette was also flat, like I could see the continents as if they were flat on a map. Simultaneously, I was watching millions of young women all working in the beauty industry. I could see them walking back and forth in the seven continents. But the incredible thing was that as I can see them in the continents it was as if I was also inside the room with each of them as well. They were so happy and disconnected from shame and regret. They were smiling and laughing. They were free!

As I'm watching this play out before my eyes, the feeling of grief changed to a feeling of obligation, of responsibility and duty. I believe the purpose for my life was revealed to me in a marvelous way that day. It was different than what I felt when I was fourteen. I believe it was different because this time, I had the resources to provide. I had the means to be able to help. When I was fourteen, I had nothing but a feeling, so I ran because I didn't have anything to offer. But now, running is no longer an option. This is my calling. My obligation. My destiny. If I run now, I would be letting so many young women down and leaving them to fend for themselves alone. I truly believe that.

When I opened my eyes, I was overpowered by overwhelming feelings. I didn't know what to say; I couldn't describe what I just saw. In fact this is the first time I've written it down in its entirety. After service, my sister Eklesia saw that I was distraught. She pulled me back into the auditorium to talk to someone. I tried to resist but she insisted.

The pastor of our Maui campus was there. I briefly explained to her what happened. I didn't get into too much detail other than saying that God was asking me to do something with my company that was too big for me to comprehend. As I started to describe this to her, I couldn't help myself, so I started crying uncontrollably again, saying, "It's too big, it's too big, it's too big, it's too big." She put her hands on my head and started praying for me, asking that God would walk me through this chapter and show me how to walk in His will.

PASSION'S STORY

After that experience, the talks with my husband about forming a nonprofit got serious. I still didn't know what to do or even where to start. But seeing what I saw in church that day, I have to be willing to walk the road less traveled. I have to fight for the young women who have had a tough go of it. I have to be ok with doing things that scares me. Forming a nonprofit terrified me but it was the fear that essentially proved to me that I was going in the right direction.

People often run from fear; for me, as of late, it seems like I run to it.

Before making the final decision to form a nonprofit, I said a prayer.

"Lord, how am I going to do this? I believe Your will
for me is to form this nonprofit, but I have no idea
where to even begin. How am I going to do this?
What will the nonprofit even do?"

A short while after that prayer, I received an email from a client that came to the salon to get her nails done. It was a feedback email to tell me she had a good experience. In it, she said that she was happy whenever she could to support local, female-owned small businesses, and mentioned if I needed help with anything, she'd support it. No big deal, right? Well, something stood out to me in that email. I don't know why but I looked up her name and what do you know, she's a consultant, a professional, and a specialist in forming nonprofits. Say what!?!

I felt led to reach out to her. I mean, come on. You can't think that's a coincidence, can you? I don't think it was. There's no way. What are the odds that this woman reaches out to me, and she specialized in the very thing I just prayed about? The first time I met her, I asked about that email, and she said,

"I don't know it was weird. Something just told me to email you that day. I normally don't do things like that."

See! I rest my case. That was my confirmation that I needed to move forward with forming the nonprofit. Oh wait, the "coincidences" don't end there.

The weekend of October 17, 2020, my church had a women's conference. The title of the conference was *Her Signature Move, Do It For Her.* There was a pastor there that gave an amazing sermon on faith. Her name is Alex Seely. In that sermon, she talked about the power we have in our thoughts. She asked the question:

"Why can you believe it for someone else, but not for yourself?"

That hit me especially hard. I'm always talking about helping others, and what I want to do for others, but not once do I consider getting help myself or allowing someone to help me. I suppose because of the past betrayals I experienced whenever I did accept help, it became harder and harder for me to accept it when it was offered. What hit different though was when she said,

"You lower your standard to accommodate your circumstance. Then you tell Jesus what He can and cannot do."

Ouch! She told us to make a demand on HIM that day, then asked us what that demand was going to be. When she asked us to come to the altar to pray, let me tell you, after the experiences I'd been having with all of this, I ran up there so fast.

My body folded over that altar, and I started weeping. I didn't want to lower my standard to accommodate my circumstance. I didn't want to doubt what God could do in my life. But I was still so confused as to *how* all of this was going to happen. I'm normally in charge of everything, but this, I had absolutely no control. As I wept on that altar, the only words that could come out of my mouth were:

"How am I gonna do it, how am I gonna do it, how am I gonna do it?"

I didn't get the answer that day on the altar, but I was grasping at the thought that I had to be faithful. Picture this, how does a person fulfill such a large calling? A global calling? The level of content creation and organization for a project that size terrified me. I'm normally so private. I never liked attention and don't ask for help. I'd have to get completely out of my comfort zone to do something this massive. Me asking God, *"How I'm gonna do it,"* made sense three days later when out of nowhere, I received a text message from a marketing manager I barely knew. He said he wanted to help me and asked if I was available to meet.

The day we met, I asked him, "What made you message me?"

He said, "I don't know; it was weird. I knew about your salon. I looked it up one day and just felt like maybe I could help you with whatever you have going on. Why, do you have something going on?"

He had no idea. I smiled! Then I told him everything. He couldn't believe it either. It's been over a year now, and he is still working behind the scenes, setting everything up for the launch of this global movement.

Do you believe me now?

CLEAR AS DAY

It's been a long time coming. It's taken hundreds of hours of planning. And believe me when I tell you that none of this is happening by chance. The original idea for the nonprofit was to pay the tuition for young women to go to beauty school. I will tell you right now that the formation of the nonprofit took one more turn before finally resting on the structure that is going to change everything.

Even as I write this book, this new thing hasn't been announced yet. The revelation didn't come to me until two years later, the day before I went to Thailand to learn about the sex slavery industry there. For years I've been saying that big things are coming. I never could quite explain what it was or what it would look like. I just felt it was going to happen. People called me crazy; some even made fun of me and gave me smirks whenever I'd talk about it. They didn't believe me. In fact, they made me question it myself. I started to ridicule the idea and count myself out. But now I can see it!

God showed me what it looks like, and it's clear as day.

20

COMMIT

CHANCES

I'm glad you came up to this part of the book. I hope it has served you well up to this point.

However, we need to have a chat. Chances are this isn't the first time you've read this type of book before, someone's story of hardship and chaos and how they made it *through*. I can say with certainty that people have given you advice on how to deal with your hardships and pull through. I haven't said anything in this book that you don't already know. Yet, you're still reading it, and I know why.

You never took the advice you were given. My question to you is, what have you learned from this book so far? Are you going to do the things you've learned? Honestly, if you know that you are not going to try to change your life, that you don't think you have the energy and stamina to face your fears and confront your past, do someone a favor and gift this book to someone you believe will implement the philosophies I've shared.

However, if you can commit to yourself, right now, that you're going to at least implement one thing from this book, I can't wait for you to turn the page. Up till this point, I've been laying the foundation for what I really want to say. If you're going to change for the better, I'm going to give you all you need to know in the next two chapters. Turn the page; your purpose awaits.

21

FIND YOUR PURPOSE

THE SHIFT

I told you in chapter four that a shift is coming. I told you that change is inevitable. I wrote this book to share with you the shift that happened in my life, in hopes that it will motivate you to find the shift that will change yours. When you find it, I encourage you to grasp it. Embrace it with all your being. I believe your shift is close. I believe you too can find your passion and unravel it. Untie the knot that has been suffocating you. Let it loose. Be a rebel for once and confront your past head-on.

DO THIS EXERCISE WITH ME

Pick the darkest moment of your youth. Do you see it? What does it look like? How long did that darkness last? Was it a day, a month, a year, or perhaps it was a season? Now, ruminate on it for a moment. Can you start to see the environment? Can you smell it? Can you hear the thoughts you were having back then? Good! Now consider this:

No matter what you've gone through, you're still alive. And as long as you're breathing, as long as there is still breath in your lungs, that little girl, or that little boy, the person you were in that dark moment in your life, is begging you to talk to them. To hug them. To meet them where they are. To simply just see them!

I know you're frustrated because you haven't become who you know you can be. I know you've been passed over, ridiculed, and counted out. I know that when you begin to think about your past, you freeze. You don't know what to say and you don't know what to think. You try to speak, but the words won't come out. And as soon as the words start to flow, the tears begin to fill your eyes.

THEN YOU STOP! You stop because you're afraid of what may come out. Don't stop!

Open your mouth and let it out. Let it all out!

Let it be bad; let it be ugly. No one cares except you. Who are you trying to hide from other than yourself? The shift in your life will not happen until you confront yourself, until you confront your past. I ran for thirty years and refused to confront my past.

Because I did that, I believe that's why my shift ended up happening in public. It was bad; it was ugly. The groans were violent and everyone around me heard my cry at church that day. That moment, although spiritual in nature, needed to happen. It was imperative that I confronted that thirteen-year-old little girl. She was desperate and needed to be seen. To be heard. And to be saved. I had to be reminded that I am still that little girl. When I found her again, I had to be asked the question, *What am I doing for the next, little girl that needs to be saved?* I had to be reminded what my purpose was.

Why was I born into my family? Why did I go *through* the hell I went through? Why was I born in such a time as this? When you confront your past, you will hear what your question is.

And it may be different than mine, but the answer will help you find your purpose.

I FOUND MINE

Purpose: what does that even mean? We hear it all the time. You've heard me say it here repeatedly. Sometimes I think when we say a word so much, it loses its meaning. Before you leave me, I don't want you to lose the meaning of what purpose means. The definition of purpose is the reason for which something is done or created or for which something exists. Here's my take on this.

- The reason for which something is done:

When I started on this new career path, I didn't have a reason for why I was doing it. It's safe to say that I started it because I needed a job and was learning that I was good at something other than property management. I figured, why not do something I enjoy doing if I'm going to do anything at all?

- The reason for which something is created:

It wasn't until after struggling to get off the ground that I found the reason for why I created Paixxão. It ultimately was to solve a problem. Well, two problems—provide training and mentoring to aspiring nail techs, while solving the sanitation concerns that clients experienced in nail salons.

- The reason for which something exists:

I've had the privilege of meeting so many amazing, young women. Sitting in the front-row seat, watching the most important part of their lives being played out has been priceless. What's even more incredible is getting to know them in a genuine way. Through providing them with the means for a way out and giving them sound counsel, I've learned that this is the reason for which I exist. I exist for this moment, this city, this career. This life!

Without these ladies and my clients, I would have never discovered who I truly am. So many times, I failed to share this part of me with them because I was afraid. I was scared because for a long time, I didn't have clarity on what my true purpose was. I repeatedly asked myself, who am I? And what am I supposed to be for these women? Regrettably, my fear caused me to lose relationships with so many of them. Fortunately, living through that kind of heartbreak is the reason why today, I'm reforming everything about myself. My environment, the people I surround myself with, and especially the way I think and make decisions.

Finally, I realized that I must create a foundation that will allow me to save the next generation of young women I mentor. I can only do that by taking care of my mental state. In order to help others, I must fill my cup first. And I believe that through this industry I can do that.

My job now is to teach others how they can find their purposes using this industry as the outlet. An outlet from unwanted lifestyles. An outlet from abuse. An outlet from slavery. And *through* that outlet, find themselves in a beautiful way, just like I did. What's astounding is that this journey doesn't have to be a career; it can simply be a steppingstone to another career; it can be a life skills development journey; it can be whatever you want it to be. And that's what makes it beautiful.

What part do you play in my mission, my vision for all of this? Why are you really reading this book?

I believe you're reading this book to learn how to confront your past and find your future. Your future may not be in the beauty industry, but do you know someone who can use it? I can assure you that you envisioned your future being a lot different than it is right now. What is your passion? Do you have one? When was the last time you asked yourself that question?

I heard someone say once that passion can be viewed as a simple question; What do you do that comes easy to you? Something that takes little to no effort to achieve? That is your passion. Now use that passion to find your purpose. Learn how you can use it to help others, or perhaps even make a career out of it. Jay Samit says in his book, *Disrupt You,* "Security doesn't rob ambition; the illusion of security robs ambitions."[1] I believe that to be 100% true.

The other reason why you're reading this book is to have a different perspective of the beauty industry. I believe you know someone that is lost or stuck and can use this business as leverage to escape their darkness. Perhaps that person, is you? Only you know that.

22

THERE'S NO I IN BEAUTY

WHY HAS NO ONE EVER EXPLAINED THE BEAUTY INDUSTRY LIKE THIS BEFORE?

I may have left this question for the last chapter, but it is certainly not the least important. I believe the answer to this question explains the true meaning of what the word beauty means in the beauty industry. Has it ever occurred to you that no one talks about the role of the client in this business? The true role.

What about the consumer that steps into salon environments day in and day out? Don't they have secrets of their own?

There's no recipe that tells us what type of person likes going to salons. You would think everyone enjoys it, but that's not always true. Perhaps you fall into one of these categories of the type of person that enjoys going to a salon.

1. Are you the person who is being pulled in a million directions, trying to help everyone else but yourself? Going to the salon is the only time you can do something for you.

2. Are you the person that longs for peace and quiet at home? But the only place you find it is at the salon?
3. Or perhaps are you the person that is living through abuse and being at the salon is the only time you aren't confronted with violence?

The salon is something different for each one of us. Often, it's a place where you don't have to pretend and are free to simply be yourself. Unbeknownst to many of us, the beauty industry is a clash of:

Two worn-out individuals that, when brought together, start an incredible healing process.

Cam, one of my team members, accommodated a last-minute nail appointment. When the client walked into the salon, she was quiet and very reserved. She was wearing a hospital band on her wrist and had cuts and bruises all over her body. When she sat down with Cam, she explained that she was just released from the hospital for swallowing glass. Can you imagine? Glass? How does that happen? Is it safe to assume it wasn't by accident?

The young lady told Cam that she only had $100 in her pocket, and she wanted to spend it on herself. So, as soon as she left the hospital, she Googled *Best Nail Salon in Albuquerque.*

She wanted to know what it felt like to treat herself, to put herself first, for once.

As she continued to share her story of brokenness, distress, and abuse, the story made Cam feel uneasy. She excused herself for a moment and came looking for me. When she found me in my office, I can tell she was distraught. She started sharing this young women's story with me and asked me if she could pay for her service.

I told her no.

Not because it wasn't a good idea. I said no because I believed we needed to honor the young women's decision to do something nice for herself. Who would we be if we took that blessing away from her? It's part of her healing process.

Instead, I told Cam the best thing she can do for her client was to give her the best service she'd ever experienced. Talk to her. Engage. Be interested in things she's interested in. Give her an extended massage. Be present! After a few minutes, I walked out to the salon and met this young woman. I engaged with her as well. I asked her what she wanted on her nails, made some suggestions for nail art, and complemented her choice. Then I put my hand on her shoulder and told her she was going to have an amazing experience.

Her smile lit up the room; she was having so much fun. It was beautiful.

People will say that a salon is just a salon. It's an appointment that should be quick. Heck, some of us are convinced that booking appointments to get nails done is silly. We tell ourselves we're too busy for that. We just want to walk in, not talk to anyone, and leave in peace. What I'm trying to say is that this thing called the *beauty industry* isn't just about outward beauty. And it certainly is not a chore.

It's about two broken people coming together, sharing stories, and saving each other. Literally!

LET'S CHANGE THE WORLD

Now that you have the full picture of what the beauty industry is, what it can be, I'm going to tell you how I'm going to provoke a revolution that will impact our culture in a gigantic manner.

But before I get to the revolutionary solution, allow me to be vulnerable for just a moment. Whilst training, mentoring and coaching dozens of young women in the past seven years, I discovered patterns. As my team grew, I saw different versions of myself in many of them. For example:

- The traumatized girl that became an expert at hiding her feelings. The nail industry for this girl was healing. It provided therapy through the relationships she built with her clients. The first client that re-booked their appointment always got me. The look on their face when they heard that someone wanted to come back to see them was priceless. It did something to their psyche. They recognized for the first time that they can be themselves and people would not only stay but they wanted to be part of their lives. They cared about what they had to say and wanted to build a relationship with them.

- The girl that was making bad decisions left and right but felt trapped. Paralysis kept her from changing her circumstance. The nail industry for this girl opened a next level type of opportunity she didn't know existed. For the first time she had options. Options that didn't require her to rely on others for. It was options, that through her hard work she unearthed. Herself! This girl, when she recognized her power, she flourished beyond anything she ever dreamed.

- Then there's the girl that built her identity on the value of one person. The minute that person wasn't around as much she felt lost and unappreciated. This girl is challenging. She possesses so much talent but often seeks validation from the person she built her identity on. To find her self-worth she needed that person *in the room*. The minute that person wasn't around she second guessed her ability. That action eventually turned to resentment. The resentment then turned to losing respect then turned into hate. Don't get me wrong, she still benefited from the nail industry and eventually found her self-worth, but the resentment left her feeling wounded. She felt like she was somehow wronged in the process because the person she valued wasn't around.

If I had to expose one crack in my company, it would be girl number three. If I'm being honest, there's a little bit of girl number three in many of the young women I've mentored.

I didn't account for these young women to need me to be in the room in order for them to feel accepted, appreciated and valued. I thought my job was to provide them the environment in which they could succeed in and that was it. I was wrong. But even being wrong, the reality is, there's only one me. Operating a large company with such a mission took me away from my clients first, until it eventually took me away from being in the building with my team. I have a heart to help, that's true, but I was running a business. I had an obligation to keep the doors open and the clients flowing so that they could succeed. If my business didn't grow, the incredible environment I created for these women would cease to exist. That's a risk I was not willing to take. But through my transition of being the nail tech to becoming the entrepreneur some people were hurt along the way.

I recognized early on, that Paixxão isn't just a nail salon. It's a company that develops young women and teaches them to use the nail industry to escape their realities. It's a company that removes all the barriers to empower them to succeed in ways they never thought possible. Although these things are good, how could I fill the cracks, resolve the faults and be immune to the kryptonite that was hurting me? What's missing? Despite the cracks and faults, I know what I created works. It's helped so many already.

Paixxão already possesses the culture that I've laid out in this book. The systems that I developed for Paixxão to change the culture are being used successfully every day. I'll tell you what those systems are:

1. The idea of only hiring beauty school graduates
2. Our in-house training platform
3. Our philosophy of development through patience
4. The beautiful design and décor, which was created not just for the clients. It was created so that my team will immediately have a sense of pride and professionalism when they step foot inside. The picturesque atmosphere makes them instantly feel beautiful themselves
5. Only using top-of-the-line products
6. Providing the team state-of-the-art equipment and tools

7. Our mentorship and coaching systems
8. The mental development we provide our team
9. The safe space we created for our team and clients alike
10. The life skills training we provide
11. The level of patience needed to build self confidence in others
12. The proven strategy and innovative approach that help others obtain success easy
13. The positive relationships we create that build self-worth
14. And lastly our core values, we are—accountable, aligned, disciplined, results-oriented, transparent, and inspirational.

The culture I built has allowed so many young women to develop, grow, and thrive personally and professionally. My methods allowed me to provoke a revolution in the beauty industry. The problem, however, is this revolution has remained within the walls of my salon.

The shift I experienced that October Sunday happened two years ago, and the intensity of that experience affects me today at the same level it did then. When God told me I was hoarding the resources He gave me, I didn't understand it.

It took two years of fighting myself before I found myself, two years of me growing *through* my difficulties and re-developing myself.

Re-learning who I am so that I can give what I've learned to others. It all makes complete sense to me now.

Paixxão IS Passion's Story.

It's been under my nose this entire time. Passion's Story is what will fix all the cracks, all the faults. It's the solution to my kryptonite, but I was too blind to see it. I didn't form a nonprofit; the nonprofit already exists. The structure is in place; all it needed was the clarity. You don't understand! As I'm writing this, this revelation is being revealed to me. Oh, my goodness, this is insane. Is this really happening to me? This is why God wanted me to write this book? For three years I refused to write this book because I didn't know where to start or what the purpose behind it even was. I'm sitting in the car with my husband as I'm writing this last chapter and he's looking at me like I'm crazy because the download I'm receiving right now is freaking me out. I cannot type fast enough. I don't want to miss one ounce of information. It's like a large cloud just dissipated and I can see so clear. Wow y'all God is amazing. There is no way I would have come up with this myself. No way! So, now what? How do I implement this? What's the blueprint? What happens to Paixxão? How does Passion's Story even work?

Ok, first Passion's Story creates a team of mentors, coaches and trainers. We employ counselors and therapists so that these young ladies have all the resources I couldn't provide all by myself at Paixxão.

Next, through scholarships, Passion's Story pays the way for them to get through beauty school. We will also assign them a counselor that will guide them through the whole process.

After they graduate, we employ them in the first EVER, nonprofit salon (Passion's Story). There they participate in a 12-month work study internship program. I'll even list the numerous reasons why this paid internship works:

- They will earn a sustainable income
- They will get on the job training
- The counselor that guided them through beauty school will also guide them through the first year of their career
- They will have access to a therapist
- Mentors will share knowledge that produce them confidence
- They will be introduced to local salon partners
- They will be coached by distinguished beauty professionals
- They will be given a customizable career plan

Can you see it? Can you see how this solves all the issues that are plaguing young women all over the world? Passion's Story is a massive steppingstone for underprivileged and underserved young women escaping perilous lifestyles, running from an abusive relationship, recovering from human trafficking or aging out of the foster care system.

Passion's Story is the outlet.

For seven years I thought I was trying to solve a local problem. But God!

WAIT! I got the revelation, but what do I do with my existing team? What about Paixxão?

Paixxão doesn't go away. You're probably wondering what I'm talking about. Bear with me, let me explain. To make room for Passion's Story I have to restructure Paixxão. But how do I do that? This shift is my opportunity to implement a system I know will help my existing team succeed further then where they are now. Now is my opportunity to take all the issues and past suggestions I've gotten and resolve the challenges we've been facing. This won't be easy; I may lose some people because you know people don't like change. But it's my duty to make room for Passion's Story. It's my obligation to make room and expand the culture I've built to make room for those that need it the most. I would be doing a disservice to young women everywhere if I hoard this information or limit it in any way. I'm forced to make decisions many people will never understand but let it be known, I'm doing it for her.

Finally, a tangible solution that closes gaps in communities everywhere. But I bet you're still wondering what happens after the 12-months.

After they've gotten all the training, have built a clientele, and are ready to fly, they will have the choice to do their own thing or go work for another amazing salon wherever they choose. Heck, it can even be in another city or state. For some, it will be the first time in their lives they have choices to choose from. I believe Passion's Story will create a cycle of success for millions of young women around the world. Someone once told me, *if you give a girl a chance, she can change the world.*

OPPORTUNITY

I'll leave you with this:

The year after the world shut down, I was invited to a girl's Sunday luncheon. You know the type, where you only know one or two people attending. I agreed to go weeks before but the morning of the event, I decided I wasn't going. I had such a long week and didn't feel like going anywhere that day. I'm an introvert, and gatherings like that can be draining for me. For hours, I was thinking of an excuse I could use not to go. Except last minute, I decided to go anyway.

And boy was I glad I changed my mind. It was a win I didn't expect. It was clear when I walked in that it wasn't just a luncheon; it was a celebration of my friend's birthday. And it was a surprise. What kind of friend would I have been if I didn't show up? After we ate, we did an exercise where each of us described what she meant to us, and then she went around the table and did the same for everyone there. There was not a dry eye in the room.

It's one of the most memorable moments I have of this friend. Totally worth the trip, and it made me feel so much better about the week I'd had. Some of you have very busy lives. Maybe you're an introvert and putting yourself out there can be draining. Or perhaps you're already thinking of an excuse not to get involved with this mission. Can I encourage you?

Despite the busyness, you decided to read this book. That's a win! This mission isn't just a vision of some small-town girl. It's a celebration; it's a surprise birthday event. We're celebrating the birth of something amazing that the world hasn't seen yet. When we're done, we will go around this table we call earth and describe what each one of these young women mean to us.

But they will go around their cities and describe what each one of us mean to them. And I promise you there won't be a dry eye anywhere.

I discovered recently that 50% of the homeless population in New Mexico are underserved teenagers living perilous lifestyles and among those are young women that aged out of the foster care system and are at risk of being trafficked. I believe I can align these two worlds. Not just in Albuquerque but everywhere. The burden of possessing this life changing system that I created has rested on me heavily as I grasped on to a deep found sense of duty to solve this problem.

There is a window of opportunity to bring this type of beauty to a city near you, in a huge way. It's an opportunity to change the culture of salons. Getting involved with this mission will do that. Every time you think about how you can help young women, now you'll know how. But do it now, not a year from now. Why wait? The number of at-risk youth is only growing.

Passion's Story is seeking out these young women to teach them how they can leverage this amazing industry. *Through* it, they can find confidence and with it, they learn how to possess self-worth. And we can help them find it because they deserve a chance at a better future.

What you are witnessing is my attempt to solve a global problem.

The decision to embark on this journey has been far from easy. For two years I have been on a course to restructure my entire company to make room for others to experience a new culture in the beauty industry. Passion's Story is not about my story, it's about theirs.

Passion's Story is not just a nonprofit, it is a movement. A movement to mobilize the beauty industry and revolutionize the way we impact a generation. This is the first of its kind, in the world, a full functioning nonprofit salon building a social infrastructure to help young women through training, mentoring, entrepreneurship coaching, financial literacy, and personal development, all while building a clientele and earning a sustainable income. Man, I haven't even started to talk about the pilot programs I'm actively working on to put beauty schools inside schools where young women as early as sixteen can start working towards obtaining their license.

This is the concrete set of resources I talked about in Chapter 9. It's tangible: it's the kind of help young women can see, feel, and touch. It's the type of help no one can take away from them. Ever! Now they have something they can look forward to and will be certain that they will have a bright future.

The revolution doesn't end there. In our social profit salons, we will have a child learning center that will dual as a child care facility so single moms don't have to choose between working and taking care of their children. This two-generation approach will empower them to strive even further and break the cycle of poverty.

Picture a day when you meet a young woman that you helped jump-start their career. Picture a day when your daughter, niece, or grand-daughter walks up to you and says, "Thank you for showing me what I can be. Thank you for showing me how I can serve and help others less fortunate." Picture a day when you look back and feel proud of what you've been able to accomplish with only your willingness to be a part of an incredible mission.

There are several ways you can help, and I encourage you to take the next step.

1. Visit www.passionstory.org and choose an area where you can volunteer.
2. If you can't help by volunteering, perhaps you can help financially by donating to this cause.
3. Recommend this book to your friends and family.
4. I'm looking for speaking engagements. If you know someone, I'd love to speak at their events, podcasts, or churches.
5. This mission will require a team of people to get it done. If you know anyone looking to invest, my email address is priscilla@paixxao.co
6. Lastly, if you own a salon or beauty school and would like training or you're looking for a mentor to teach you how to

implement the systems I created, please don't hesitate to contact me. You can find me on my website www.iamPriscillaSmith.com.

This mission serves a global purpose. I may not be able to paint you the picture in one book as to how big it's going to be, but you've seen how God has shifted my life in ways I could never comprehend. This mission is not by chance; it's a God-driven mission, and whether you believe in God or not, our job here on earth is to find our passion, unravel it, and give it back.

It's time we recognize the hope we have in our youth! Will you join the Mission?

I pray that your hearts will be flooded with light so that you can understand the confident hope He has given to those He called.

— EPHESIANS 1:18 NLT

ACKNOWLEDGMENTS

First and foremost, I'd like to thank God. Without Christ, none of this would be possible. Next, I'd like to thank Danny, my husband. During our twenty-two years of marriage, you have dealt with a lot. Me trying to find myself and dealing with all my past hurts. You flawlessly have displayed all the fruits of the spirit written in Galatians 5:22-23, love, joy, peace, patience, kindness, goodness, faithfulness, gentleness, and self-control. Without you I wouldn't be here to write about my story and how it's going to impact a generation of women. Love you baby!

I'd like to thank my three kids, Nakqi, Brielle and Deja. Thank you for being good well-mannered children with big hearts and willing to help mom in helping others. You're young but all three of you are mature for your age and will do amazing things in your life. I know it! Be brave, mom loves you very much.

To my parents. I know life wasn't easy. But I know you gave it your all, you're still giving it your all. You provided me with more than I could have asked for, a Godly example of marriage and character. Much of what I went through wasn't your fault. It was the decisions I made that took me down paths you didn't want. Thank you for never giving up on me and praying for me without ceasing. I love you.

Thank you to all my siblings. Thank you for believing in me and knowing that I would pull through. I look up to you in a unique and personal way to each of you.

A special thanks to my sister Eklesia for reminding me that I had it in me to speak to that little girl stuck inside me begging to be seen. You know the conversation, I heard it loud and clear sis. To me you're still a rock.

To my friends and my team, those that have stuck by me from the beginning, you know who you are. Thank you from the bottom of my heart.

NOTES

3. I AM WHO I AM

1. Merriam-Webster Dictionary online, s.v. "creed," accessed December 2, 2022, http://www.merriam-webster.com/dictionary/creed.

8. MY FAITH SAVED MY LIFE

1. Merriam-Webster Dictionary online, s.v. "provide," accessed December 2, 2022, http://www.merriam-webster.com/dictionary/provide.

15. CHANGE

1. Grant Cardone, author of, The 10X Rule: The Difference Between Success and Failure, published by Wiley 111 River Street Hoboken, NJ 07030, published April 26, 2011

16. MY PURPOSE STARTED TO UNFOLD

1. Merriam-Webster Dictionary online, s.v. "through," accessed December 2, 2022, http://www.merriam-webster.com/dictionary/through.
2. Merriam-Webster Dictionary online, s.v. "process," accessed December 2, 2022, https://www.merriam-webster.com/dictionary/process.
3. Merriam-Webster Dictionary online, s.v. "period," accessed December 2, 2022, https://www.merriam-webster.com/dictionary/period.

21. FIND YOUR PURPOSE

1. Jay Samit (@jaysamit), "Security doesn't rob ambition; the illusion of security robs ambition. – Jay Samit, DISRUPT YOU! Twitter, 6:01pm, September 19, 2015, https://twitter.com/jaysamit/status/645357018467794944?s=12&t=Q9AvYGXbKY-DO8iVadAPH3A

Made in the USA
Middletown, DE
07 March 2023

26318380R00110